STARTING   OUT   RIGHT

STARTING OUT RIGHT

Nurturing Young Children as Peacemakers

KATHLEEN MCGINNIS
and
BARBARA OEHLBERG

A Joint Publication of

 **The Institute for Peace
and Justice**

and

A Meyer-Stone Book
CROSSROAD • NEW YORK

1991

The Crossroad Publishing Company
370 Lexington Avenue, New York, N.Y. 10017

© 1988 by Kathleen McGinnis and Barbara Oehlberg

Cover design: Evans-Smith & Skubic, Inc.

Cover illustration: Catherine Cleary

Manufactured in the United States of America

Library of Congress Cataloging in Publication Data

McGinnis, Kathleen
    Starting out right : nurturing young children as peacemakers /
Kathleen McGinnis and Barbara Oehlberg.
      p.   cm.
    Bibliography: p.
    ISBN 0-940989-16-6 (pbk.) : $9.95
    1. Parenting — United States. 2. Parenting — Religious aspects —
Christianity. 3. Interpersonal relations. 4. Peace.
    I. Oehlberg, Barbara, 1932-   II. Title. III. Title: Children as
peacemakers.
    HQ755.8.M44   1988
    649'.7 — dc19   87-20982
                                                           CIP

Just as the twig is bent,
the tree's inclined.

—ALEXANDER POPE

Contents

Acknowledgments

There were many people who helped create this book by their willingness to comment, offer suggestions, and share their own stories. To all of them we owe our gratitude. We want to acknowledge particularly the loving support we've received throughout this project from our husbands, Dick Oehlberg and Jim McGinnis. Also, our special thanks to the people who have taught us our parenting skills and refined them through many years of patience and laughter — our children, Mark, Kurt, Mary, Chris, Sarah, Eric, and Paul Oehlberg, and Tom, David, and Theresa McGinnis.

Preface

"This is interesting, but I have a three-year-old! What does this mean to me?" "How do we begin?" "What are some important things to keep in mind in the earlier years for my children?" "Can my child start to develop peacemaking skills before school age?" "What are young children capable of?" These are some of the questions parents of young children are asking, parents who are interested in peace and justice and want to see ways to link that interest to their own parenting skills, as well as parents whose initial interest is in parenting but who are open to looking at parenting with an eye toward the broader world. In this book we are attempting to tap into the vitality, the enthusiasm, and the real thirst for knowledge that are often characteristics of early parenthood. We also apply some basic educational and parenting strategies that have been explored and explained in other contexts specifically to the very young child. Parents of pre-school-aged children (weary though they often are) are also often exceptionally receptive to fresh insights and new angles on old pictures and are themselves fertile ground for creative growth.

We came to collaboration on this book because of our mutual trust in the imagination and creativity of parents and because of our passionate belief that peacemaking concepts and skills can be tenderly nurtured in very young children. We have both been active for some time in the Parenting for Peace and Justice Network. Kathy and her husband, Jim, coordinate the Network from the office of the Institute for Peace and Justice in St. Louis, Missouri. Barbara has served as a coordinator in the Ohio region since the Network's inception in 1981. The Network is a loose-knit association of families of all kinds who seek "Shalom" — well-being, wholeness, peace, justice — in their own living situations as well as in the broader community. It seemed especially appropriate to both of us that we draw on our own parenting and educational experiences to bring the same vision that infuses the Network to bear very concretely on the parenting of pre-schoolers.

Barbara is the mother of seven children, ranging in age now from twenty to thirty-three. As a parent, when she reflects on nurturing peacemaking skills in the very young, she is both looking back and looking forward. As do all parents, she wishes that she had had access to other insights and alternative methods when her own children were toddlers and pre-schoolers. She also looks ahead very immediately to being a grandparent and to the renewal of spirit and ideas that will come for her as she begins "grandparenting for peace and justice." Barbara has been active for a number of years in the peacemaking programs of the Presbyterian church as a member of Swords to Plowshares of the Western Reserve Presbytery. Her concerns about peace and justice have been nurtured through that group as well as through OPEN (Ohio's Peacemaking Education Network), and CEASE (Concerned Educators Allied for a Safe Environment). Through these associations and her professional work as an early childhood and parent educator, Barbara has developed and refined her insights into what is possible with very young children.

Kathy's children are now teens — thirteen, fourteen, and seventeen. While her active parenting of pre-schoolers is in the past, her concerns about the specifics of nurturing young peacemakers are very much in the present. Kathy and Jim have been working at the Institute for Peace and Justice since they established it in 1970. Their social conscience had been sharpened and given edge throughout the Vietnam era, especially through the person of Dr. Martin Luther King, Jr., and the social teachings of their Roman Catholic church. The Institute and their family began in the same year, and in many ways the missions of both have always been intertwined. All three McGinnis children (Tom, David, and Theresa) are adopted; Theresa's Black and Native American (Winnebago) heritage has called forth some of the insights reflected in the chapter on developing healthy racial attitudes. Kathy's work in the classroom, with her own children, and as a parent educator has convinced her of the necessity of concentrating on the groundwork for future generations of peacemakers that is at the heart of working with pre-schoolers.

Both of us have made contributions to all parts of the book. The basic authorship of the chapters, however, is divided: Barbara wrote chapter 1; Kathy the remaining chapters. We both are very excited about the suggestions reflected in these pages. Our hope is that they will provide a springboard for further ideas for all of us engaged in the wonderfully challenging journey of parenting and peacemaking.

Chapter 1

Foundation Blocks

Amy is four and Suzy is three. Amy has been building a tower of Lego blocks. Suzy comes in, and for several minutes they work together in the building process. Then Suzy decides to knock down the tower. Amy pushes Suzy down. Suzy hits Amy. Screaming, hitting, and biting follow.

The names, ages, and circumstances vary, but the situation is familiar to parents.

The idea of parenting peacefully with pre-schoolers at home may strike some as incredible. At the least, it suggests lofty expectations, especially if we equate peace with quiet, for parenting with pre-schoolers is rarely quiet.

Nurturing peacemakers and agents for justice begins in early infancy. This first chapter will focus on suggestions for fostering in our children the foundations for a life of dedication to justice and peace: nurturing self-esteem, developing social relationships, and building independence and self-discipline.

NURTURING SELF-ESTEEM

The development of self-esteem is crucial for several reasons in the overall task of nurturing young peacemakers. First of all, it is impossible for any of us to function effectively without a strong sense of self. Teachers, counselors, psychologists, and psychiatrists all attest to the fact that low self-image has a dramatic impact

1

on a child's ability to function well in school and in the broader society.

Second, self-esteem is necessary to be able to care for others. No child can be compassionate toward people who are hurting, whether they are homeless in our cities or starving in Ethiopia, unless that child first of all feels secure and content about who he or she is. To reach out to others with charity, as well as sometimes with a sense of outrage about the causes of the pain and victimization, requires a secure self-image base.

Third, a strong sense of self is necessary in order to act in a public way, to do anything that is risky. During Gandhi's years in India, part of the overall Gandhian program involved setting up schools where children would begin to develop the skills necessary to be part of a society involved in social change. The curriculum in those schools included daily opportunities for public performance. The children would come to an all-school assembly to play musical instruments, recite poetry, sing songs, and tell stories. The philosophy behind this was that the children needed opportunities to act publicly in order to develop their own sense of self so they would not be hindered by self-consciousness in contributing to the larger society.

Peacemaking involves many endeavors that involve some element of risk, whether it is stating that you disagree with someone, signing a letter to the editor of a local newspaper, breaking up a fight on a playground, or marching in a demonstration. The solid base of self-image that is begun in early childhood can enable older children or adults to do something they feel is important, even though there is a risk involved. Often the stands or actions they feel called upon to take will put them in a position where they are different from others around them, and to be different requires a strong sense of self.

And finally, self-esteem is essential in dealing with difference, whether that difference is racial, religious, or economic. Bigotry and hatred flourish in the minds and actions of people who have a low sense of themselves and therefore must find someone else or some other group to be a scapegoat or to "keep down." Learning to live in a diverse society is an essential task of peacemaking.

But how does all of this apply to very young children? What are specific ways we can nurture self-esteem in their lives?

Trust and Basic Needs

We can begin with the solid development of *trust* during infancy and the toddler months. So essential for positive self-esteem to emerge later, trust is first nurtured by the manner in which the basic physical needs for touching, caring, and food are met. Infants can sense how they are valued and loved by the promptness and gentleness with which their needs are met. Since infants have never experienced a sense of "future," the moment of crying is the "eternal moment" in which they feel helpless and abandoned. After all, there were no delays or loneliness *in utero!* If you've ever waited for service in an emergency room for three or four hours, you can imagine how an infant might misinterpret several minutes of delay.

Each time that we as parents feed, diaper, cuddle, or burp our babies we are building their trust level and laying a foundation for self-esteem. Of course, as our babies grow into toddlers and older pre-schoolers, they continue to need to have their trust cultivated. They need to have assurance that their basic needs will continue to be met — food, body contact, warm clothes, attention to scrapes and bruises. With such assurance they can then feel secure about dealing with the rest of their environment.

Validating Feelings

Our willingness to respect and accept our children's feelings will enable them to accept and trust that part of themselves. Children three and under do not have the fully developed verbal skills to express their feelings to us, but they are masters at candid, uninhibited body language. It is often easy to deduce their emotional state from their body language. They need our acceptance of their feelings, even though they have not been able to label them.

We may want to assist our child in verbalizing what we sense he or she is feeling. We can offer words to match their body language — always, of course, in a non-judgmental manner, for example, "I guess you might be feeling..." or "You seem to be feeling...." Or we might tenderly suggest they might want to go to their room to spend some time quietly with their feelings. Or perhaps they would like to share their feelings with a favorite doll or stuffed animal. We can offer to go along to be with them in their own quiet place. The message we want to convey is that our love for them is constant even when they are angry, scared, or jealous.

Another way to help our youngsters learn to feel comfortable with their own feelings, as well as those of others, is to comment on what we witness together. Let's say, for example, that while we are shopping we both observe an adult who completely "loses it" with another person and screams uncontrollably. As the child absorbs it all with mixed fear and confusion, provide the words that might help him or her to process the experience. "He must be very angry. I wonder if the yelling is going to help them settle their differences. How do you feel about watching it all?" Using the words "I wonder" makes it much easier for children to respond since it permits them to tap their imaginations rather than requiring them to come up with facts.

Preparing our children for experiences that may generate fear or uncertainty is also valuable. We can "design" the experience by using toys, constructing a mock-up, or role-playing, for example, a first hair-cut or dentist appointment and then talking about feelings the experience might generate. When engaging in a role-playing or "what-if" scenario, parents might ask, "What could you do for yourself at such a time to feel safer or stronger?" Provide an opportunity to express these or other feelings once the event has taken place so that they can work through their memories.

Be alert to "testing" questions or comments long after you might have expected an event to be forgotten. The tragic explosion of the *Challenger* is a case in point. A totally unrelated story six weeks after the event triggered one five-year-old boy, much to the surprise of his father, to bubble forth his real feelings about it. The boy brought the subject up daily for a week afterward until he had worked his way through it and was able to move beyond the memory.

The following family activities are designed to help our children accept and feel comfortable with a full range of human emotions and feelings.*

- *"The Book About Me":* In order to love, our children need to feel lovable. To help them feel important and special, we can offer to help them create a book that tells all about who

---

*Many of these activities are taken from *Exploring Feelings*, by Susan B. Neuman and Renee P. Panoff (Atlanta: Humanics, Ltd., 1981).

they are. On the cover boldly print (for them, if necessary), *The Book About Me,* followed by their name. Succeeding pages can be dedicated to various aspects of their lives, either through their drawings or their words, printed by us exactly as they have dictated. Have pages entitled: My Friend, My Family, My Favorite Food, My Favorite Drink, My Favorite Fruit, My House, My Favorite Animal, My Pet(s), The Time of Day I Like Best, My Favorite Clothes, My Favorite Book, My Favorite Song, My Favorite Gift, I Am Happy When..., I Am Sad When..., When I Was a Baby I Liked to..., Now I Can Do....

- *"Simon Says It with Feeling":*

    Simon says: "Show that you are surprised to see a present on your bed."

    Simon says: "Show that you are mad because your dog ate your favorite book."

    Simon says: "Show how you feel when your dad drives into McDonald's."

    Simon says: "Show how you feel when your brother gets a cookie for picking up all the toys."

    Add your own....

- *"What's This Person Feeling?":* Find magazine photos of people and ask your child to identify the feeling expressed by the person in the photo. Or have your child guess the feelings that you act out. Or let your child act out a feeling in front of a mirror and you guess the feeling being demonstrated.

- *Communicating Feelings without Words:* Discuss ways our bodies communicate how we feel: Tapping our feet or our fingers, wrinkling our noses or foreheads, hugging, sighing, or clutching hands.

- *Expressing Anger Constructively:* Old sock or mitten puppets with angry faces on one side and happy faces on the other are very useful. Encourage children to pretend that the puppets are characters in one of their own experiences. (This can be done with one child and two puppets or with two children.) Allow them to re-enact an angry scene. Encourage them to use words to tell clearly how angry they feel. You can guide without judgments. When feelings are worked through, turn the puppets around and allow the happy faces to complete the reconciliation.

When you feel comfortable about guiding this process, use it to explore how your child feels after incurring the anger of parents. Talk about how your child feels when parents are angry, how the love between you is always there but how angry feelings sometimes make it hard for all of us to feel loving and lovable.

- *"I Get So Angry When... ":* Look into the mirror and make angry faces. Together draw angry faces on paper plates and discuss how sometimes we are afraid to share our angry feelings. But there is nothing wrong with being angry, so say so!

  Put a paper-plate mask in front of your face to lead into a sentence-completion activity: "I get angry when...." Talk about how we feel better after telling someone how angry we feel.

- *"I'm Angry!":* Stuff an old pillowcase with rags and tie it closed. When your child is angry invite him or her to wrestle with it or punch it to release tension (not to avoid resolving conflict).

- *Feeling Disappointed:* Ask your children to mention times when they have felt disappointed, when an experience did not have as happy an outcome as expected. Examples: a picnic was ruined by rain; the store was closed when you got there; you were detained and so you could not go out together as planned; a friend had a cold and could not come over to play. Talk about how they felt. Then talk about experiences that were satisfying and happy.

  Tell them you have a make-believe magic box (use a shoe box) filled with millions of things. Let each child open it and pretend to take something disappointing first, then something relished. You may have to help — "Oh my, look! You have a great big onion as your present! Are you happy or disappointed?" "Let's try again. Wow! Now your present is a new bike!"

  Stress that moments of disappointment are inevitable, but so are moments of joy.

- *"Sometimes I Feel Scared":* Talk about how we all feel scared sometimes — when we are alone, at night, in new places. Note that when we talk about what we fear, we do not feel so alone anymore. Discuss ways you could ease these feelings of fear.

- *Special Cards:* Make personalized cards for special folks in your child's life. Discuss the person to be honored; elicit facts about that person and the feelings your child has for him or her. Ask, "How does grandpa show you that he loves you?" "How do you feel about your sister?" "What kinds of things do you like to do with Aunt Sylvia?"

  Encourage your child to "describe" his or her feelings with colors and lines (crayons) to decorate the card after you have printed your child's comments on it. Then deliver the card to the special person.

- *Family Interview:* A family interview session, perhaps while traveling, is another group affirmation activity. And it makes a fine tape to send to a distant grandparent. Each member of the family is asked:

  Can you remember a time you made someone else really happy? Tell us about it.
  How did this make you feel?
  What was the happiest day you can remember?
  When were you really brave?
  When were you the happiest to get back home?
  When were you really scared?
  When were you able to stop a fight or an argument with words?
  How did you feel?
  What has been your greatest discovery or creation?

- *Intergenerational Family Networking:* Seated in a circle at table or on the floor, roll a ball of twine or yarn from one person to another. The receivers have to respond to the question for that round. Holding on to the string, they roll the ball to another family member. Questions for each round:

  The best thing about this family is...
  The most fun I have had with our family was...
  I am proud to be a part of this family because...
  The job I like to do with our family the most is...

(Add what seems appropriate.)

After several rounds, comment on the network of strings across the circle, how it holds and connects you all within the "fabric" of your special family.

DEVELOPING SOCIAL RELATIONSHIPS

Sharing

Sharing, or rather attempting to meet the expectations of adults regarding sharing, will probably become your young child's first hands-on experience with justice — and injustice.

This age group considers everything they touch as an integral part of themselves, literally as a part of their body. If they are asked to share their favorite toy with another child, it is like being asked to give up an arm or a leg — an actual part of oneself. Imagine how confusing this could be for children, particularly when a loved and loving parent asks that of them!

These are painful moments for parents as well, because they often occur when friends or relatives are present. Naturally, we become aware of our image as effective parents. But the need to be seen as a successful parent is our need and not the responsibility of our child. At that moment our child is experiencing his or her own painful need for affirmation of worth.

At such moments children desperately need parents as advocates. A two- or three-year-old is not capable of managing such situations, nor of meeting the expectations of well-meaning adults. Before total disintegration occurs, why not redirect the child's interest or remove the child from the situation? A hasty trip to the kitchen or bathroom for a "needed" drink just might save a vulnerable, tender ego as well as the self-esteem of the parent. Sustain your child's opportunity to remain in harmony with his or her positive self.

Children never question the expectations of adults, even truly unrealistic ones. Their only deduction is that they do not measure up.

Between the ages of three and four children can begin to "practice" sharing and to understand the concept. Not until after their fourth birthday will most children be able to feel comfortable and natural about sharing.

Enhancing Social Self-Confidence

The full-time occupation of older pre-schoolers is improving personal and social skills through play. Play for the pre-schooler is learning to learn. As three-year-olds' interest and participation in social play increase, their ability to interact productively with age-mates has a direct impact on their sense of competency. The feedback from playmates now becomes very important toward enhancing their self-esteem.

Before age three, most children enjoy being with other youngsters but will interact sparingly. Most play is parallel play at this stage. By age four most youngsters have begun true cooperative play in groups. Experiences and skill gleaned during this period will determine whether or not they will continue to choose cooperative group behavior.

The social skills learned in group play are important because our children's future is with their peer group. To survive they need to master skills for negotiation and conflict resolution. Because their relationships are based on equality, only peers can teach these skills to each other. But, as parents, we can guide these learning experiences and help our children "process" or reflect on their interaction.

When parents resolve problems *for* their child, they in effect communicate that children are not capable of solving problems, a notion that may linger well into adulthood. For some of us, that may be one of those absolutes we've carried in our minds since our own childhood, a logical deduction if our parents or teachers always solved our problems for us.

Parents can provide young children with opportunities to learn to trust their ability to solve problems by asking them questions that will permit them to "discover" an answer. Introduce to them the awareness that answers are already in their minds. The key is asking the questions that make it possible for children to answer them.

Non-judgmental discussion openers might include, "You seem to be having a problem playing in the sandbox. I wonder what you might do so both of you have fun?" Children who have been empowered to trust their ability to discern alternatives avoid perceiving themselves as helpless and are free to choose cooperative behavior.

When self-affirmation is insufficient to gain influence with play-mates, over-assertiveness emerges. Children who feel incompetent or incapable of influencing others may resort to extremes in order to exercise some control over peers. Children who are bossy or contentious are often that way because of their own sense of pow-erlessness. Conversely, children who believe in themselves are able to be democratic in their use of influence.

How can we facilitate our children's belief in their own com-petence? This guidance can be in the form of helping our chil-dren re-process social interactions once their equilibrium has been restored — sharing some juice and fruit would certainly get this started. We can initiate the reflective processing by suggesting, "I wonder if there might have been some other way that situation could have been handled?"

We might also want to be aware of our inadvertent parental involvement in sibling tensions. Are our children's arguments ex-clusively theirs, or are we fulfilling the third person or "point" role in the triangle, thereby promoting tensions between siblings?

Such a scenario is always easier to spot in a neighbor's family than our own. Pre-schoolers themselves can identify such triangles but need guidance toward solutions. I recall the comments of a young playmate of one of our children who was about to return home. As he slowly put on his boots he mused in wonderment at how he and his brother never fought when a baby-sitter was caring for them.

Fighting and Power

Sometimes children may have to fight, but encourage them to stop aggression with words, when possible. Our challenge is to assist our child in "processing" these situations by asking, "What other words could you have used to stop her?" "What other choices might you have considered?" "How do you feel now about the incident?"

Most often fighting represents unsuccessful or mismanaged at-tempts to exert influence or power over another. Every functioning human yearns for power — pre-schoolers *and* parents. Power itself is not the culprit; it's the attempt to achieve it by extracting it from another because of a dread of being powerless.

Pre-schoolers, who are aware of their limited ability to exert influence on others or generate changes in a sometimes scary world managed by adults, do have real needs to experience power positively. They often dramatically demonstrate this by their fascination with superheroes.

Costumed dramatic play that relies upon imagination affords children an opportunity to discover their own internal courage. TV cartoons that graphically provide all the answers for children can leave them bereft of trust in themselves. Through imaginative play, guided when necessary, pre-schoolers can begin to crystallize their own positive power, not be frightened by it.

Other ways pre-schoolers can experience a positive impact on their environments is by playing with wheeled toys to achieve speed, by pouring sand or water (especially down ramps), and by generating noise. Additional possibilities are discussed below in the section on "Toys" in chapter 5. Unfortunately, none of these activities is likely to make the demonstration of power seem positive to parents or grandparents! But accepting the needs of pre-schoolers for a sense of power may help us deal with the behaviors generated.

BUILDING INDEPENDENCE AND SELF-DISCIPLINE

Providing Choices

Without a doubt, the favorite word of children under four is an emphatic "No," and "Me" is a close second. Those of us who can recall the sudden transition of our docile toddler into a defiant mini-general may well remember the sense of total inner resistance it generated in us. With the advice of "hang tough" from well-meaning friends and relatives ringing in our ears, it is easy to launch into a pattern of continuous confrontations during this period.

Most children under four are totally egocentric, which means they are aware of only one reality — their own. They are incapable of understanding someone else's point of view. This singular perspective may frequently put them out of harmony with parents and, particularly, with siblings. Young children need to have their interpretations accepted and respected, unrealistic as they may be. We need to respect the mistakes that are the result of incompletely developed skills.

PEACE TABLE
Conflict resolution with young children

Goal: To provide children an opportunity to be heard and understood. If this method is used for punishment it *cannot* work.

The Only Rules: (1) Everyone must touch the table to talk, adults too! (Children love it when adults must touch the table.) (2) No one can say what has already been said!

- Any table can be a Peace Table.
- Any place and any time.
- The adult is the negotiator.
- Children involved in conflict come to the Peace Table and tell what happened from their point of view.
- Anyone can add to the presentation of the problem.
- After the problem has been stated from all points of view, the children are asked to give alternatives on how the problem could have been solved.
- The adult helps the children develop concrete solutions or alternatives, e.g., a child says they should be nice to each other; the adult asks how. The adult restates options to the children, never saying which option they should take or what to do, never asking them to say they are sorry or force adult solutions on them.
- The adult can ask the children to applaud themselves for being Peacemakers and give special peacemaker stickers or badges to the offended.

Time: Approximately ten minutes.

Children have no problem listening or staying involved because they learn after the first time that they are full participants. I have used the Peace Table in my classroom for three years. Children soon call for the Peace Table themselves. Many children have initiated the Peace Table in their homes, neighborhood play, and in other schools.

— Adapted from Dolores J. Kirk

As parents, we can begin building our young child's ability to re-evaluate situations by discussing alternatives: "What else could you have done to help the situation?" "What would you like to see happen?" "How do you think your friend Tommy is feeling now?" "How do you feel about the misunderstanding now?" The goal is not to come up with the "right" answer but to encourage our children to generate as many possibilities as they can. Also, by focusing on feelings, we can avoid judgment of anyone.

Giving children a choice is very important in these situations. Choice allows young children to learn how to ask themselves essential problem-solving questions. We can facilitate the process by helping them put the choice into words: "What would make it possible for you to put on your boots?" "... sit quietly in your car seat?" "... put the toys back on the shelf?" Firmly state what the desired action is but inquire precisely what they would like to have happen so that they can proceed.

By involving young children in this way we imply that they have the ability to take responsibility for their action. (In situations of real danger, of course, our approach has to be modified accordingly.) By coaching our child in the mastery of this problem-solving process, we are providing a tool for non-violent conflict resolution.

Children, even pre-schoolers, can tell the difference between meaningful, productive choices and manipulative options. "Eat your squash or go to bed!" is not a true choice; it invites choosing between being obedient and disobedient, and this is not a productive choice for child or parent. Repeated counterproductive or unjust dilemmas can lead children to choose disobedience and result in family power-struggle patterns.

How often do our "rules" initiate creative misbehavior rather than thoughtful compliance? My children are now quite candid as adults and frequently reveal surprising truths as they recall childhood memories. These occasions are usually very humbling for my husband and myself; we thought we had been effectively managing their behavior all those years. One of our rules was that everyone had to taste the vegetable at dinner to qualify for dessert. Some twenty years later we learned that one of the girls had been slipping the two or three green beans placed on her plate for tasting into her socks and then flushing them away when visiting the bathroom.

Because young children cannot separate themselves from their behavior, it is very difficult to criticize their actions without upsetting their ability to remain in harmony with themselves. Our best chances of nurturing self-esteem are to "design" our children's environment so that they maintain equilibrium. We should guide our children into successful experiences and remove them from possible devastating experiences before they occur.

We can prepare the pathway to positive learning experiences by redirecting our children away from inappropriate behavior; get them interested in something else, offer an alternative "discovery," or simply pick them up and move them to a different room.

Guidance Toward Self-Discipline

With guidance and encouragement from parents and family, self-discipline will emerge in our children concurrently with positive self-esteem. Like self-esteem, self-discipline must be generated from within, nourished by successful experiences. As much as we might like to, we cannot, as parents, "teach" or superimpose self-discipline on our children; they must decide to develop it for themselves, by themselves. Self-discipline cannot be nurtured without choices; without choices there is only obedience.

As language skills emerge, parents might want to offer opportunities for their child to gain a workable understanding of the words used in problem-solving. During the third year we may want to coach our child in the words essential to considering consequences. Help a child internalize the sequence of "If . . . , then . . . ," and "Why . . . ? Because. . . . " We can practice these as we read stories to them or watch TV and ponder together what might happen before we turn the page or how the commercial will end. These words are the tools for associating consequences with behavior and are the stepping stones to responsible behavior; they teach our children how to think rather than what to think.

At about age four, children begin to realize they can initiate actions and behavior, that they and others can be accountable for results. In fact, the four- to six-year-old becomes quite preoccupied with the notion, new to them, that there is a correct and an incorrect way of doing things. For the first time children begin to understand that if they indeed can decide to do something, that is, initiate action, then they are responsible for the behavior they enact and the positive and negative consequences of the behavior.

This is a tremendous step and one that permits children over four to extract meaning from learning experiences, the essential bridge to becoming responsible and self-disciplined.

This new level of understanding is closely followed by the realization that there can be alternative viewpoints that have value and validity. These understandings are essential for thinking through consequences and, in general, mean the pre-schooler is now ready to deal productively with verbal guidelines and rules.

For the first time in the child's short life, clearly defined rules enable growth in awareness of competencies. Rules can now become a criterion for successes.

Processing negative experiences or failures can help our child learn from them, but we don't need to bring them up again and again. We might ask, "What else do you suppose you could have done?" or "What other ways do you think you could have tried?" Generally, children (and parents) will experience negative learning situations because of a lack of skills, not because they are obstinate, mean, or willful.

"Time-out," as a disciplinary tool, can be expanded into a productive learning experience. After a negative incident, request your child to report to you, before returning to play, some other ways he or she might have acted. If the incident involved another child, require your child to report what that other child might have enjoyed or appreciated more than what actually happened. This process helps children focus on alternatives that parents can then guide.

To raise children who will champion justice, they must first experience justice. Try to reserve rules to the absolute essentials of good health and safety, and then make certain that your child fully understands the rules and the reason for them. We also need to make perfectly clear what the consequences of failing to abide by the rules will be.

Dr. Steven Glenn has a marvelous suggestion for ways to help children become aware of the association between their behavior and the consequences they experience. The time to initiate this step is during the pre-school years.

Let's say we have a household guideline that before the children watch their favorite (and approved) evening TV program, the toys in the family room must be cleared and stored. The corresponding consequence is no TV if toys are not cleared. If the guideline is not followed, a parent announces, "I gather you aren't planning to watch TV tonight. I respect your decision."

This process enables children to realize how their own choice has created the consequence they are experiencing and prevents the deduction that mom or dad is the cause.

These "foundation blocks" — nurturing self-esteem, developing social relationships, building independence and self-discipline — are the layers that undergird and support all the other skills and concepts that are part of the peacemaking picture. The chapters following will look at other elements of that picture — healthy racial attitudes, dealing with sex-role stereotyping, attitudes toward older people and people with disabilities, dealing with violence and war, and the faith dimension of all of this — always with the conviction that attention to the foundation blocks is crucial and has immediate carry-over into all the other areas.

Chapter 2

We're All Different! : Healthy Racial Attitudes

Once I had a funny dream.
Everyone was just alike,
and nobody was different —
just like paperdolls.
I wouldn't like that!
Everybody in the whole world
is different.

Nobody's exactly like me.[1]

It was a lovely summer day, and Sarah had taken her three-year-old son Mark to an amusement park close to St. Louis. They were on a "River Raft" ride, which used a Huckleberry Finn theme as its central focus. It was dark, and as Sarah and Mark came around the bend on their "raft," a huge "Injun Joe" figure popped out, complete with tomahawk and war paint. Sarah remembers Mark being frightened, but his fright didn't seem to have any lasting impact on him. That evening, however, as she was giving him his bath, suddenly Mark said, "I'm glad I'm not an Indian." Sarah was startled, and asked him why. His response was immediate, and she knew it was directly connected to the incident that afternoon: "Because Indians are mean and they kill people."

We would like to believe that our young children are not as yet affected by the ugly realities of racism. We would like to be

convinced that our pre-schoolers live in a world where skin color is
not a barrier to friendship and understanding, where all children
feel good about their own racial identity, and where equality and
sharing among races exists. But real life intrudes on our preferred
vision of our young child's world.

Social science research continues to assert that very young children are influenced by the attitudes and behavior of the society
around them with regard to race. One of the landmark studies on
racial attitudes in young children was done by the anthropologist
Mary Ellen Goodman in 1952. Her study focused specifically on
four-year-olds and her main conclusion can be summed up in these
words: "It [white over brown]...is the most comprehensive idea
to which our children are exposed. The idea is pervasive and it
pervades silently, like a creeping fog, and is just about as difficult
to stop."[2] Even though that study was done thirty-five years ago,
the tragic truth is that more recent studies have reached the same
conclusion.

In 1978–80 Louise Derman-Sparks, Carol Tanaka Higa, and Bill
Sparks did a study in Southern California that dealt with children's
attitudes on racial identity and racism. A report on their study
was published in the *Bulletin* of the Council on Interracial Books
for Children. When discussing pre-schoolers the researchers state,
"Three- to five-year-olds are still learning to determine what is
authentic and what is not; stereotypic and inaccurate images and
information are therefore particularly harmful at this age."[3]

Perhaps more important for parents than social science data,
everyday life suggests the same truth.

Cheryl's mother has vivid memories of an incident that occurred when Cheryl was four. Lynn, the mother, had been
talking with her about some of the other children in her
pre-school class. When she mentioned one little girl's name,
Cheryl's reaction was immediate: "I don't like her because
she's Black." Lynn was dumbfounded, and after some gentle questioning was surprised to hear Cheryl say, "But Mom,
she's different from me." One of the reasons for Lynn's surprise was that Cheryl had an adopted biracial brother. Later
on in the conversation between Lynn and Cheryl, when Lynn
asked directly about what color Cheryl thought Eddie, the
younger brother, was, Cheryl answered unhesitatingly, "Oh,

he's brownish, mostly white." Reflecting back on that incident, Lynn felt that the "mostly white" was an important distinction for Cheryl, even at that early age. Even though Lynn knew that a major developmental task for pre-schoolers was differentiating, especially with regard to self, she still felt that the racist attitudes of society had had an impact on her child.

Beulah, a Cherokee mother and grandmother, works with many Native American people as an employment specialist in a large urban area. She says that over and over again she sees Native American children beginning school with bad feelings about themselves, fearful that other children will discover that they are Indians. The teasing and name-calling that they must endure seems to be based not only in a "brown over white" mentality, but also in specific stereotypes in other children's minds about Indians.

An experience in our own family brought the reality of stereotypes home to us with startling clarity. Theresa was only a year old and Tommy was five. I was talking to Tommy about Theresa's Native American heritage, about what it means to be a member of the Winnebago Nation. He listened patiently to my explanation. Then he looked up and asked, "Mommy, when Theresa grows up will she kill us?"

We think back to that incident often. It was a startling indication to us of how deeply ingrained stereotypes, misconceptions, and fears can be, even at a very early age. Tommy, who at that time did not know any Indian people besides Theresa, had a very clear and very negative idea about what Indians do to people. We thought we had screened out sources of negative attitudes, but we had not.

Race is basically a social rather than a biological concept. In today's world it is very difficult to say exactly what "race" some people belong to purely from a biological perspective. I know a child whose father is Chinese and white and mother is Black and Filipino. What is that child's race? Tragically, the social system in the United States has functioned in a way that says that the lighter you are the better. But if you have any Black heritage at all, then you are decreed Black and are unable to enjoy the "privileges" of white society.

In other words, race in U.S. society has tremendous social, political, and economic implications, and children begin to get some
insights into that at a very young age. For example, even though
they cannot make abstract judgments, they do begin to notice that
most wealthy people are white and that many people of color are
poor. They also begin to notice the absence of people of color in
certain environments or situations. This is particularly true, of
course, if they are used to racially mixed situations. So a white
five-year-old who has always gone to church with only whites would
probably not comment on that. But a white five-year-old who was
used to an integrated church would definitely notice if she were to
go to a church where the whole congregation were white. I can
remember one of our children remarking at a very early age that
all the Shriners in the opening parade at the Shriners Circus were
white men. She wanted to know why that was the case. There
are times like this when a simple question by a four-year-old can
initiate a discussion of how racism manifests itself in various institutions in our society.

Because pre-schoolers are excellent observers, the "color-blind
mentality" makes little sense. It is not helpful to young children to
say directly or to imply that they do not see color. In fact it may
give the child the feeling that differences in skin color are negative,
and that adults somehow wished those differences weren't there.
Pre-school-aged children know that people are different — in skin
color, hair, eyes, etc. They do not automatically interpret those
differences to be either negative or positive. This is not to say that
children are always comfortable with differences; they are not. To
deny that differences exist, however, is to deny the obvious to a
child.

This does not mean that it is advisable or even possible to be
constantly and consciously referring to those differences. A teacher
with a class of three-year-olds need not be thinking as her morning
goes on, "Now, there are three Black and two white children in
the block corner, two Vietnamese children at the dress-up corner,
four whites and two Black children playing with puzzles. . . . " But
she does know whether or not she has Black, Vietnamese, or white
children in her class.

Similarly on an interpersonal level, when I am taking my daughter, who is Black and Native American, and her friend, who is
Vietnamese, to the store, I am not thinking, "I have a Vietnamese

and a Black–Native American child in the car with me." I am only aware that I have Theresa and Casey in the car with me. But there have been times when we've had moments of "racial recognition." We will put our three arms next to each other and comment on the different skin tones or we will talk about the differences in our hair. The basic task for us as adults then is to lay the foundation for children to begin to interpret differences in a positive rather than negative light.

It seems obvious that the racial realities of the larger society in which we live have a bearing on the budding racial attitudes of our very young children. The key question for us as parents and other nurturers of young children is how we can make a difference in our children's lives. What can we do, given the state of the world outside our home?

I would like to separate the answers to that question into two broad categories — "Adult Strategies" and "Strategies with Children." By "Adult Strategies" I mean specific suggestions about how we can look more consciously at our own attitudes, behavior patterns, and responses to individual situations. "Strategies with Children" will include suggestions about what to do with very young children to initiate and develop positive racial attitudes.

ADULT STRATEGIES

Taking a look at our own racial attitudes and behaviors is far from an easy task, but it is essential if we are concerned that our children's attitudes and behaviors be healthy.

Our Own Background and Past Experiences

The following questions can help us look at our own past and present:

- What is the racial composition of the people with whom you work?
- What is the racial composition of the neighborhood in which you live?
- Have you attended any racial awareness workshops or training sessions in the past three years?

- What has been the racial character of your educational experiences? (Racial identity of fellow students, teachers, etc.)
- Have any previous living or working experiences put you in contact with a significant number of people from a race other than your own? (If there are many of these experiences, list just the most recent three.)
- List some of the people, educational experiences, books, etc., that have contributed to your own positive sense of racial identity. If you are a person of color, who and what have made you feel good about your own racial heritage? If you are a white person, consider who or what has made you feel good about your ethnic background (Irish, Italian, Polish, etc.), as well as who or what has given you a better sense of what whites have done to contribute to racial understanding.
- Name one person or experience that has had a significant positive effect on changing your racial attitudes.[4]

Informing Ourselves

An important part of dealing with our attitudes toward our own racial identity as well as toward other racial groups has to do with our degree of accurate information about racism, race relations, and the history and culture of various racial groups. A very basic strategy, therefore, is to set up for ourselves some kind of program of "information-gathering." Suggested resources are listed in the resource pages.

Looking at Our Everyday Relations with People

Young children's observation powers are keen, and they are tuned in to body language as well as to tone of voice and more subtle reactions that we as adults express toward other people. Therefore, if they sense that our reaction to another person is one of warmth, openness, and friendliness they will feel that that's what their response should be. This is not articulated, but is an emotional response that can provide a foundation for more reasoned responses later on. Conversely, if children experience anxiety, coldness, or even hostility from us, the foundation for a generally negative set of attitudes has been laid. This can be true even in infancy. Dr.

Phyllis Harrison-Ross and Barbara Wyden relate an incident in their book *The Black Child:*

> Charlie was five months old, blond and blue-eyed, alert and active. He seemed to love everybody. Anyone who smiled at Charlie got a smile back, and sometimes an excited waving of arms as if he wanted to show how delighted he was. His mother had taken him to the pediatrician for shots, and now they had left the office and were getting into the "down" elevator. Lois was startled to find a man in the elevator. He was Black. Suddenly she was conscious of everything she had read and heard about drug addicts and muggers.
>
> "Should I ring the alarm bell?" she wondered. But why? What would she say? The man wasn't doing anything. He was just standing there smiling at her baby.
>
> Lois wasn't aware of it, but her heart was beating faster; her grip on little Charlie had become uncomfortably tight. Charlie, who had been staring at the Black man with great curiosity (this was the first Black face he had seen), did not return the man's smile.
>
> Lois took this to be some sort of indication that Charlie sensed that the man was dangerous. And she became more nervous. As the baby twisted uncomfortably, trying to loosen his mother's grip, he looked at her face. It wasn't the face he knew. His mother's lips were pressed tight; there was a tenseness in her face that changed its look. Charlie cried. The face he knew was soft and loving. What was this tense face, this altered heartbeat that he felt as if it had been his own? Charlie began to cry.
>
> All this took place in seconds. The elevator door opened on the ground floor. The episode was over. Lois shushed Charlie, cuddled him a little, told him what a brave boy he was to have all those shots and be so good. Lois didn't give a second thought to the episode in the elevator. But she should have. She had just taught her baby to regard Blacks with fear, anxiety, anger and hostility.[5]

It is extremely important that our children experience us in friendly, warm, giving relationships with people of various racial groups. They learn a lot by observing us, in our own homes or in other social situations, with people whom we call friends. They also learn from our interactions with people on a more casual basis — at the grocery store, in the doctor's office, on the bus.

Sources of Humor

Racial and ethnic jokes and cartoons are not new. What is relatively new is an increased understanding of the effects of these sources of humor on the thinking of very young children. If a three-year-old hears an adult, especially a parent or teacher, tell a joke that has racial or ethnic overtones, that child will internalize the foundation for an attitude of triviality and negativity with regard to the people who are the focus of the joke. Whether the basis for the humor is physical characteristics, intelligence, language, cultural traditions, or method of conducting business, the result is not a positive one for a young child. While the children will very seldom understand the joke, they do understand the general attitude behind it. They know that the person or group of people is being "made fun of."

When our daughter Theresa was about four years old, we passed a Pontiac dealership one day while on our way to Grandma and Grandpa's house. The dealership had a huge sign on the side of the building with a caricatured, befeathered Indian complete with an oversized beaked nose saying, "Me Heap-Em Big Trader!" Even before I told her what the words were, Theresa knew immediately that the picture was "making fun of Indians." That was exactly what she said to me and was the reason why she said she didn't like the sign. Explaining to our pre-schoolers that we don't like those kinds of jokes or comic strips or cartoons because they make fun of people is the basis not only for a more positive overall attitude but also for critical-thinking skills at a later developmental stage.

Dealing with Racist Incidents

Overt racist behavior, whether name-calling or exclusion because of race, can be a very traumatic experience for a young child. I remember quite vividly explaining to our pre-school children why the word "nigger" was absolutely forbidden in our house, describing it to them as a hate word. But often more than explanations about specific words is required. The Cambridgeport Children's Center in Cambridge, Mass., has drawn up guidelines for dealing with

racist incidents. Below are excerpts that have particular relevance
to parents:

Observe:

- How many children are involved? Who are the victims, vic-
  timizers, bystanders, or observers, etc.?
- What other factors might affect the situation beside racial
  conflict/discrimination; e.g., sex differences, age differences?
- Was the incident precipitated by conflict over toys, space,
  etc., so that the issue of sharing should also be discussed?

Respond:

- Let the children know that discriminatory behavior, name-
  calling, etc. are not tolerated and that sharing and cooperative behavior will operate to their advantage.
- When a child has been victimized, make that child feel sup-
  ported.
- If other children have witnessed or been peripherally involved
  in the incident, it is important to involve them in the process
  of responding to the incident.
- Determine if it is necessary to separate children and talk to
  them individually. Sometimes the most appropriate action
  is to take the "victimizer" aside to discuss her/his behavior, especially if the intended victim was not aware of the
  discriminatory comment or action.
- Try to turn a negative situation into a positive one; for instance, turn exclusion into sharing.[6]

STRATEGIES WITH CHILDREN

The enthusiasm, energy, and generally upbeat attitude toward people that characterize the early years make the ideas we try with
children very rewarding. Children during the pre-school years want
to like people, to have everyone be their friend, and to relate openly
to others. Suspicions, fears, anxieties, and hostilities based on race
are not intrinsic to their psyches. Keeping that in mind, we can
have a high level of assurance that whatever we do will have a
reasonable chance of success in the long run.

This is not to say that, given the realities of racism today, it will be an easy task to set our pre-schoolers on the path toward positive racial attitudes. But it is to say that there will be positive effects from whatever we try with our children, even if the results aren't evident to us for years to come. When my teen-aged children say to me, "Mom, you'd like this TV show. It's about people fighting against prejudice," I feel that maybe something has rubbed off. When a friend tells me that her daughter, who is white, was uncomfortable in a new high school because of overtly racist remarks she was hearing from other white students, I think that that family's foundation in the early years has had an impact. So we come to the question: What can we do with our pre-schoolers to start them on the road to healthy, positive racial attitudes?

Visual Images Around the Home

Pre-school-aged children are very visually oriented. They pick up values and unstated messages from pictures and other things they see in the home. Therefore, it is important for them to see a variety of skin colors, racial features, hair styles, and dress depicted in their own home. In a young child's mind, these images, while not real people, represent some degree of acceptance by the adults in the home. In other words, the child begins to develop the attitude that it's okay, possibly even good, for people to look different from each other. These "people," as it were, have been brought into and accepted in the child's own home.

Also, particularly for children of color, there is a direct connection to self-image. John and Sylvia, a Black couple, have their home filled with pictures of Black people. They feel that their sons are not going to get that kind of self-image reinforcement from school or from the media, so it is of paramount importance for them to provide it at home.

This does not need to be an expensive endeavor. I cut out a picture of Martin Luther King, Jr., from a calendar one year, framed it, and gave it to the family as a Valentine's present. It was interesting to me that our son David, nine years old at the time, was particularly impressed and walked around the house to find just the right "special" spot for the picture. He wanted a place where everyone could see it.

Toys

The selection of toys is a major project for parents and others who nurture young children. Geraldine Wilson, author, early childhood educator, and consultant to schools and parents, puts the challenge this way:

> Do you want toys that engage and fire children's imagination in constructive ways? Do you want toys that encourage thoughtful, rapt involvement? Do you want children to become independent and actively involved? If you think toys ought to embody and/or symbolize values that are human, anti-racist, anti-sexist and cooperative and that encourage and reinforce justice and concern, then you will have to have a sharp eye and choose carefully, for most of what you would like to buy, most of the gifts that will do those things might not even be in toy stores. But, look carefully at what is in toy stores. One, you will receive an education; two, most toy stores do have some surprises — toys that you can give children in good conscience.[7]

We will have more to say about toys in the chapters on sex-role stereotyping and violence/war. For our purposes in this chapter, we want to concentrate on the impact of toys on the formation of racial attitudes. We want to offer several criteria that we hope will be a help in selecting toys that promote positive racial attitudes and in becoming more critical of toys that send out negative messages with regard to race.

Does the toy, simply by its visual imagery, give the child a sense of the variety of peoples that make up the human family?

There are some Black dolls now, as well as occasional Black children pictured on toy packages. Still rare is an image of an Asian, Hispanic, or Native American on a toy or toy package. Native Americans are often prey to stereotypical images (tomahawks, war bonnets, feathers), but are practically non-existent in any accurate way. In an informal survey of toys for children five and under in a nearby "Children's Palace," I found the following:

• The images on toys and toy packages are overwhelmingly white. I found only one out of twenty dolls to be Black in our toy store, with no Hispanic, Native American, or Asian dolls.

There are such dolls, but their availability is not widespread. Buyers have to know what companies to seek out and which stores to patronize. One company is Golden Ribbon Playthings, 575 Madison Ave., New York, NY 10022, which has a wonderful line of Black and Hispanic dolls — "Huggy Bean and Family."

- Boxes and other toy packaging were even more white than dolls. I found one Asian child on a Sesame Street package, one Michael Jackson puzzle, one Black child on a Fisher-Price toy, one Black and one Native American in the Fisher-Price little people, several Black boys pictured on a basketball set, and one football autographed by a Black player. Admittedly, my research was not exhaustive, but I was surprised and disappointed by the disproportionate percentage of white images, particularly on infant toys, where I did not find one non-white image.

Even very young children can begin to develop the basis for critical-thinking skills. They aren't yet capable of skills like analysis and evaluation, but if we say something like, "I wish there were more Black dolls in this store," or "I think they should show children of all colors playing with this toy on the outside of the box," we plant the seeds for a more critical level of thinking.

Does the name given to the toy itself or to characters that make up the toy present a picture of the variety of peoples in the human family?

Dolls and other toy characters need to have names that are derived from a variety of racial and ethnic perspectives, rather than solely Anglo-Saxon names. It is a learning experience for a child simply to play with a doll named Yolanda, Katsura, Keshia, Luce, or Casimir, or to play a game with similarly named characters. Parents can encourage children to use a variety of names when they are naming their own dolls or characters or even stuffed animals. It is true that children often like to name toys after people they know. Depending on the child's environment, those names may be fairly restricted, but our suggestions themselves can give them the idea that there is a broader world signified by different names, even if they decide on the names more familiar to them.

Do the games available promote cultural understanding?

There are in fact games on the market whose origins are in

a variety of cultures, including Third World cultures — e.g., the mathematical game Owari (from many different African nations) and Chinese puzzles. Pointing out these origins to children is a simple way to expand their horizon.

Puzzles that depict positive images of Africa, Asia, the Caribbean, the South Pacific, or Latin America are difficult to find but worthwhile hunting out.[8]

Reading

Children's books are important conveyors of messages about people and the society in which we live. The bibliography in the resource pages includes books that we feel will add to young children's positive feelings about their own racial identity as well as other racial and cultural groups. There are four criteria that were used in selecting the books listed:

1. They present authentic information about elements of different cultures.

2. They directly counter racial stereotypes.

3. They depict children and/or adults of different racial or cultural groups in non-stereotypic ways in everyday situations and settings.

4. They offer positive role models or heroes from different racial or cultural groups.

Some of the books include several of these elements, while some incluide only one or two. The numerals 1, 2, 3, or 4 after the name of a book refer to the four factors listed above (see the resource section listed below, pp. 115–117).

Stories

"That's not right! She should be able to sit where she wants on the bus. And she was tired!" With those words a four-year-old summed up with remarkable clarity the central point and the real humanity in the story of Rosa Parks. Mrs. Parks was the Black woman whose refusal in 1955 to accept segregated seating on a Montgomery, Alabama, bus was the impetus for the bus boycott, a key element in the beginnings of the Civil Rights movement of the late 1950s and 1960s. Our young children relish these kinds of stories whether we read to them from books or just tell them stories familiar to us. Effective multiracial education can take place through the retelling of stories of people who have been and are prime movers in the struggle for racial equality. Some biographies are suggested in the children's reading list in the resource section. People whose stories can be interesting to young children include:

Mary McLeod Bethune	Rosa Parks
Paul Robeson	Harriet Tubman
Jackie Robinson	Chief Joseph
Fannie Lou Hamer	Grimke Sisters
Langston Hughes	Daniel Inouye
César Chavez	Sojourner Truth
Alicia Alonso	Dr. Martin Luther King, Jr.

Other kinds of stories, or fantasy trips, are also important learning opportunities for children. Peg, a white mother who adopted a Vietnamese child, explained something she did with her daughter to give her a stronger sense of her own racial identity and cultural heritage:

... This was an imagination game in which Kris and I were on a boat that just left St. Louis, and we were sailing to her special country, Vietnam. I'd ask her to imagine what it would be like when our boat got there. It was always just a little sailboat and we would accidently come to shore and a whole bunch of people would be there.

In this imagination trip we talked about the weather being pretty warm.... People would probably wear wide hats to keep the sun off of their faces.... Their skin may be dark, but their hair would be like Kris's and their eyes would slant, just like hers.

Then we'd try to imagine what it would be like if a little girl asked Kris and myself to her home to eat. We'd talk about homes on wooden legs to keep them high, away from flooding water... eating rice with vegetables... using chopsticks.

This kind of story is directly tied to adoption, but similar fantasy trips could be conceived for "visiting" many countries. The key to Peg and Kris's trip was a deep respect for the people and the imparting of knowledge not influenced by stereotypes and geared toward an appreciation of specific differences.

Television

Even though many of us consider television an unwanted intruder in our home, there are programs that play a positive role in the formation of healthy racial attitudes. For young children, "The Cosby Show" is the best example currently on the air. "Sesame Street" also has elements that are very good in terms of characters, music, and specific cultural appreciation. Watching these shows with our children enables us to comment favorably on what we see and reinforce the positive messages.

Conversely, shows that have negative or stereotypical images also need to be discussed. I remember watching a cartoon show with one of my children. The show depicted Native Americans in a stereotypical way — befeathered, chanting war hoops, and carrying tomahawks, looking for someone to scalp. A simple comment from me — "I don't like this because it makes fun of Indians" — prompted a discussion with my four-year-old son. Even though he had no conceptual understanding of stereotypes, he did understand that the show was making him feel uneasy about Native American people. (I do have to admit that as our children have gotten older, they have not always been so eager for our "critical comments." There have been times when they've said, with a sigh of frustration, "Mom, we *know* this is a stereotype. Can you just leave and let us watch it anyway!")

Dramatic Play

Pre-school-aged children love to be involved in the telling of stories through drama. The impact of the story is also greater when they are more directly involved in it. Four-year-olds understand quite readily how to interpret through drama the story of Rosa Parks. Jackie Robinson's struggles and triumphs in major league baseball, César Chavez's battles over the rights of farmworkers, Alicia Alonso's breakthrough in the world of ballet, Harriet Tubman's courage and ingenuity in the operation of the Underground Railroad — all of these are wonderful themes for dramatic play for young children.[9]

People in Our Home

One of the most important sources of learning for our children is the modelling they see in their own home. One aspect of this is the group of people whom our children call our friends. It is significant for them to see a multiracial group of people enter our home. This encourages them to make friends with children from races other than their own.

Color Associations

Various factors can engender either a positive or a negative mind-set in a young child regarding skin color and associations with different colors of skin. Part of this process is a reflection of cultural language patterns. The English language has many more positive definitions for "white" than for "black." Parents can offset this reality by offering positive images for dark colors and avoiding negative ones. In their book *The Black Child*, Dr. Phyllis Harrison-Ross and Barbara Wyden give specific suggestions for parents of Black children, some of which apply to all parents. Following is a brief excerpt from their guidelines:

> I like to see mothers pat a child's cheek and say, "You've got beautiful brown skin." I like to see a wife rub cheeks with her husband and say, "You're as Black as an African king." Or a father tell his daughter, "You're just about the same color as Aretha Franklin. And a lot better looking. . . . "
>
> Make your child color-conscious. Explain how people come in a variety of colors. And how much people like color. Talk about what colors he or she likes the most. "Would you like a red sweater or a blue sweater?" "Do you want to wear your yellow socks this morning? Yellow's a bright happy color like the sunshine." "Oh, you'd prefer your green socks because they make you think of the green grass in the summer." Talk about the colors of flowers. Your child should come to understand that there are many shades of color in this world and that all of them have their place. "Oh, you don't like brown? That's strange. I always think of brown as the color of the good earth that gives us our food and all the flowers we like. And I think of brown as the color of the

big brown bear that prowls through the forest. And I think of brown as the color of chocolate milk, and I know you like that, don't you?" And black? It's easy to avoid talking about the color black, but it's not a good idea. Show your child the night sky and talk about how the stars shine in the velvety black sky, just like diamonds or pieces of glass. Or talk about the black ink that comes from the pen and the black print of books and how black has always carried messages to people, given them ways to learn and think. If you have a black telephone, there's no reason why you can't refer to it as "my Black friend who keeps me in touch with the world."[10]

Another way to look specifically at the skin color question for children is to be very intentional about describing differences in skin color — all with positive associations:

Some people are black like ebony wood.
Some people are light brown like roast turkey.
Some people are pink like bubble gum.
Some people are brown like chocolate cake.
Some people are white like vanilla ice cream.
Some people are yellow like a ripe pear.
Some people are reddish brown like cinnamon rolls.
Some people are tan like peanut butter.[11]

A beautiful poem by an anonymous author illuminates the importance of positive color association for Asian people. It's a poem that could be read to young children, accompanied by pictures of Asian people.

YELLOW

Yellow is the warmth on your back
    on a cold winter day as
    you sit very still feeling it grow right through
Yellow is the daisy pushing up to the sky
    only to be stopped short, you think
    but it has really touched that sky, but
Yellow can be running scared, or
    just tainted with dust and age, or
    sour lemons, or gilded bananas, but

Yellow is the cream of the crop
as wheat fields sway in time, or
as ripened corn waits to drop, and
Yellow is the flashing light that brightens
a room, or a night, or
a mind, or a life, and
Yellow is you and me, not traces
always yellow, not always knowing
but proud we are together, yellow faces.[12]

Professionals

People who serve our families in professional and highly skilled capacities have an impact on our children. They see people whom we go to for help as "important people." We do not always have choices in these areas. But when we do have a choice, we recommend that at least one of our criterion be the following: "What influence will my choice have on my children's racial attitudes? Will it help them see people of color as competent, knowledgeable, intellectual, and caring individuals." This includes, for example, nursery schoolteachers, dentists, doctors, counselors. It has been our family's experience that an additional benefit from these choices is that Black professionals often have a largely Black clientele. That creates opportunities for casual exchanges in doctors' or dentists' waiting rooms that give children a feeling of easy familiarity, acceptance, and common bonds. (Everyone is afraid of the dentist chair!) This same situation is often true for Hispanic, Asian, and Native American professionals in areas where there are large populations from those groups.

Discussion of Racism

Pre-schoolers cannot understand the causes or the internal workings of racism. They can, however, understand the effects of racism. When our son David was four and our daughter, Theresa, was three, we had a startling experience. We were preparing to leave the house to go to the county jail in our area to visit a prisoner. The children were going to go with us, and before we left, David asked where we were going. We explained to him very simply that this young man, who was Black, and his family had moved into an all-white suburb several miles from our house. The community into which the family had moved was very hostile and very clear about wanting the family out. Shortly after the family had moved in, Gerald, the son, was arrested by the police and accused of murder. We knew the attorney who was defending Gerald, and through extensive conversation with this attorney, we were convinced that Gerald had been framed as a threat to his entire family. We had become interested in his case and had visited him a few times in jail. David listened carefully and asked a few questions.

About five minutes later, Theresa came downstairs as we were heading out the front door. She asked the same question as David had. Before either my husband or I could speak, David explained to her in a few brief sentences what had happened and why we were visiting the jail.

The most amazing thing to us was that he had the story basically correct. Of course, he did not say, "This is racism," but he certainly understood the reality. These kinds of discussions with very young children are the beginnings of a more developed understanding at a later age.

All of these strategies represent realistic possibilities for us to develop positive racial attitudes in young children. The important thing is for each one of us to feel that there is *something* we can do. We can't do everything, but at least we can start and hope for the fruition of what we're doing in the years to come. In some way we can be participants in the dream of Dr. Martin Luther King, Jr.:

> I have a dream that one day on the red hills of Georgia the sons of former slaves and the sons of former slaveowners will be able to sit down together at the table of brotherhood....
>
> I have a dream that my four little children will one day live in a nation where they will not be judged by the color of their skin but by the content of their character....
>
> I have a dream that one day down in Alabama...little Black boys and little Black girls will be able to join hands with little white boys and white girls as sisters and brothers.
>
> I have a dream today.... [13]

Notes

1. Norma Simon, *Why Am I Different?* (Chicago: Albert Whitman & Co., 1976), p. 30.

2. Mary Ellen Goodman, *Race Awareness in Young Children* (New York: Collier MacMillan, 1952), p. 90.

3. Louise Derman-Sparks, Carol Tanaka Higa, Bill Sparks, "Children, Race and Racism: How Race Awareness Develops," *Bulletin,* Council on Interracial Books for Children, vol. 11, nos. 3 and 4, 1980, p. 7.

4. Kathleen and James McGinnis, *Parenting for Peace and Justice* (Maryknoll, N.Y.: Orbis, 1981), adapted from material on pp. 60–61.

5. Dr. Phyllis Harrison-Ross and Barbara Wyden, *The Black Child* (New York: Berkley Publishing Corporation, 1973), pp. 59–60.

6. Patricia Simmons, "Handling Racist Incidents: A Case History," *Bulletin,* Council on Interracial Books for Children, vol. 11, nos. 3 and 4, 1980, p. 20.

7. Geraldine Wilson, "Toys Are Political, Too: A Guide to Gift-Giving the Year 'Round," *Bulletin,* Council on Interracial Books for Children, vol. 11, no. 7, 1980, p. 5.

8. Ibid., pp. 6–7.

9. In addition to the books in the bibliography, a source of background reading for adults is a wonderful reader entitled *Embers: Stories for a Changing World* (New York: Council on Interracial Books for Children, 1983).

10. Harrison-Ross and Wyden, *The Black Child,* pp. 109–110.

11. Mary Beth Gallager et al., *Educating for Peace and Justice,* 5th ed. (St. Louis, Mo.: Institute for Peace and Justice, 1976), p. 46.

12. Anonymous, "Yellow," in *Asian American Women,* a journal published by Stanford University, 1976, p. 46.

13. Dorothy Strickland, ed., *Listen Children: An Anthology of Black Literature* (New York: Bantam Books, 1982), pp. 76–77.

Chapter 3

Growing Up Equal: Sex-Role Stereotyping

And then all that has divided us will merge
And then compassion will be wedded to power
And then softness will come to a world that is harsh and
   unkind
And then both men and women will be gentle
And then both men and women will be strong.... [1]

Sarah was almost two and her brother Michael was four. Michael had been given a doctor kit as a gift, and the two of them were about to play with it. Very quickly a fight broke out over who was going to be the doctor and who the nurse. Michael insisted that it was possible for Sarah to be the doctor, but under no circumstances was it possible for him to be the nurse.

The expectations of our society about how men and women behave permeate every aspect of our lives, from the intimacy of personal relationships, to school curricula, to TV advertising, to earning power in the job market, even to the unstructured play of pre-schoolers. These expectations and the structures that support them (media, government, church, schools, employers, etc.) have a definite impact on the attitudes and behavior of our very young children.

   In the last ten years there have been significant changes in sex-role expectations and the ever-widening horizons for both boys and girls. It is clear, however, that sex-role stereotyping and sexism itself have a firm hold on our everyday lives as well as on the trends and patterns that shape our society. In 1984, the median annual earnings for full-time, experienced women workers was 65 percent of those of men, up only 4 percent in the last twenty-three years.

We are also aware of the rising level of violent behavior among men in this country — much of it criminal behavior. It is blatantly apparent that there is a growing attitude in our society — among both men and women, but especially among men — that supports violent resolution of conflict, both domestically and internationally. Sexism and sex-role expectations do have an impact on our everyday lives, as well as on the security of the world.

Several definitions are important as we begin to look more closely at sex-role stereotyping and the young child. We are using "stereotype" to mean "an untruth or oversimplification about the traits, characteristics, behaviors of an entire group of people." [2] Sex-role stereotyping, therefore, refers to misperceptions or oversimplifications or false beliefs about someone based on that persons's sex. Examples of sex-role stereotyped thinking that apply specifically to young children include:

- boys need to pursue more independent exploratory tasks than girls do
- appearance is more important to girls
- girls are more nurturing than boys
- boys should have more opportunities for active play
- boys should not be encouraged to play with dolls or with household articles
- block play is not as important for girls as for boys
- girls need more help in performing simple tasks

Our definition of sexism is "a system of attitudes, actions, and institutional structures that subordinates women on the basis of their sex." Secondarily, sexism also operates in a way that limits and thereby oppresses men. But the primary oppression is that which affects women.

The Council on Interracial Books for Children further explains this in their book *Human and Anti-Human Values in Children's*

Books: "We see the primary victims of sexism as women because they are subordinated in an institutionalized way, as well as by cultural forces. The sexist oppression of men comes mainly, though not exclusively, from cultural forces. We can therefore define sexism primarily as the systematic oppression and exploitation of human beings on the basis of their belonging to the female sex. Secondarily, we see sexism as the repression of people based on cultural definitions of femininity and masculinity, which prevents both sexes from realizing their full human potential."[3] In other words, while both men and women are limited by sexism, women are the ones who are left powerless economically, politically, and legally.

Another phrase related to expectations for and behaviors of young children is "gender identity" — one's self-awareness and acceptance of being female or male.[4] Alice Honig in an article for *Young Children* explains it this way:

A little boy may know that he is a boy, and feel comfortable about it, but still enjoy some activities such as playing house or pretending to nurse a doll tenderly, activities which have been considered typically feminine. These activities do not necessarily mean that he does not like being a boy, nor that he is insecure about maleness. In fact, sometimes persons who show extremely sex-stereotypic behavior and seem very uncomfortable about activities considered typical of the other sex may actually be more insecure in their gender identity than others who are less rigid in their beliefs and values about sex-appropriate behaviors.[5]

Cathy is a mother who definitely believes that children should not be confined to gender-specific roles. For Christmas she bought a kitchen set for her two-and-a-half-year-old son Patrick — complete with a small-scale stove, sink, and pantry. Her reasoning was very simple: "He needs to begin to understand that this is work that not only women do." (Patrick loved the set.)

Given the pervasive realities of sexism outside, as well as inside, our homes, what realistically can we as parents do? Our suggestions again fall into two broad categories: Adult Strategies and Strategies with Children.

ADULT STRATEGIES

Looking at Our Own Attitudes

As with any issue that we want to tackle in the world outside ourselves, the beginning point in dealing with sexism and sex-role stereotyping is within. All of us have been acculturated in a society that permits and supports unequal treatment and unequal expectations of men and women. Some of us, because of our parents' values, religious beliefs, school experience, or any of a number of other influences, are less restricted by sexist attitudes than others. But all of us bear the imprint of sexism in some way. It is essential, therefore, for us to take time to reflect on our own attitudes and the source of those attitudes. One way to do this is simply to look at a list of words and to ask ourselves whether each word makes us think of a woman or a man. Consider these words:

strong	power
babies	teacher
weeping	supportive
decisive	boss
logical	secretary
compassionate	minister
endurance	pouty
athletic	risk-taking

After noting which words remind us of women, men, or both, the next step is to reflect on the source of the attitudes, e.g., are women the only ones we've ever seen taking care of babies? Have all our ministers been men?

Another way to examine our own thinking is to look at hypothetical situations and speculate on our own reactions and the reasons for those reactions. For example:

Clint is four years old. His favorite color is pink and if allowed to pick a jacket for himself, he will pick a pink one. You are his parent. What is your response, and why?

Maria is three years old. Her pre-school teacher calls and says that Maria always wants to play with boys in her pre-school class. She seems to avoid the girls and generally chooses garb that is more typically male from the dress-up corner. The teacher is concerned. What is your response, and why?

Looking at Our Behavior

We must examine not only our thinking, but also our actions. Certainly our children learn much more from what they see us do than from anything we think or even say to them. As Letty Pogrebin puts it,

> Let Father get the dinner while Mother and the bo⸱ ⸱ play. Those idyllic images of the woman approvingly watch ⸱g her "men" cavorting beyond the kitchen window as she ⸱crubs the grass stains out of yesterday's play-clothes or warms the soup for their lunch are propaganda for woman-as-spectator. Your daughter is more likely to want to be a woman if it doesn't mean giving up the action for a view from the kitchen window.[6]

Our everyday activities speak the loudest about our true beliefs on appropriate behavior for men and women. The following list of questions is taken from *Christian Parenting for Peace and Justice* and was originally adapted from *Non-Sexist Childraising* by Carrie Carmichael. It is a list geared toward our reflection on everyday activities. The questions themselves reflect a presumption of a two-parent family or a family in which there are fairly constant male and female role models (grandparent, aunt, uncle, older sibling, etc.). A single parent could reflect on what kinds of tasks he or she suggests to children as "appropriate" for men and women.

Who stays home when the kids are sick?
Who calls the sitter?
Who deals with the school and teachers?
Who decides how money is to be spent?
Who shops for the food?
Who prepares the meals?
Who disciplines?
Who does the cleaning?
Who does the laundry?
Who fixes broken toys, bikes, etc.?
Who shops for the children's clothes?
Who soothes and snuggles the kids?
Who dresses the kids?
Who changes the diapers?

Who gets up in the night for a feeding?
Who coaches the kids' teams?
Who takes the kids to school?
Who takes the kids to the doctor? dentist?
Who gives out the weekly allowance?
Who reads to the children?
Who attends games or meets when the children are on the teams?
Who does outdoor activities with the children — sports, sledding, biking, etc.?
Who is the volunteer for school-related activities — for example, Scouts, PTA, room parent, etc.?
Who mends clothes?
Who is the caregiver when a child is ill?
Who oversees toilet training?[7]

Asking these questions is not intended to give the impression that there are clear "right" answers.

When my husband and I answered these questions, we discovered that there were many household and child-care tasks that we shared, like cleaning, taking the children to the doctor and dentist, driving the children to their activities, soothing and snuggling, and disciplining. But we discovered that many other tasks fell into the traditional molds: Jim does most of the minor household repair work, auto repair, and bike repair; I do the cooking, laundry, mending the clothes, shopping for the children's clothes.

A problem we see in our patterns is that the tasks that are nurturing and care-giving (cooking and laundry especially) are also the ones that can be perceived by the children as the "serving roles." They are tasks that fulfill the children's simple everyday needs. So we fear an association, perhaps only unconscious, between women and serving — that it is the job of women to serve others. So we struggle with how to show them on a day-to-day basis that serving need not have a gender attached to it, that the serving roles in the household are to be shared, just as are any other opportunities to nurture and care for each other.

Time, skills, levels of enjoyment are all factors in deciding how each household should run. Another factor is the degree of comfortableness with change. Several women who are friends of ours have spoken quite openly about wishing that the division of responsibilities in their homes could be more equitable. They would like not to have the ultimate responsibility for the running of the house with specific tasks given out to others in the family. They would like that overall responsibility to be shared. But they feel that their husbands and their families are not at a point where they would be comfortable with any more change.

Change is often difficult for all of us, especially when the change intrudes on our everyday living patterns, affecting our most unguarded moments, and coming at times when we are tired and just do not feel like being part of a movement for equality. Sensitivity and a deep level of communication are essential when dealing with issues that touch our deepest emotions, our very sense of who we are.

While the same could be said for every topic that we deal with in this book, sex-role stereotyping and sexism demand in the case of a two-parent family that husband and wife be especially willing to listen to each other. They need to spend the time it takes to work out patterns that are truly freeing for both, and in which they can support each other.

Another aspect of our looking at our own behavior relates to the kinds of interests we are developing for ourselves. Do our interests (and specifically, of course, those interests that our children see us pursuing) reflect a wide variety of skills, abilities, and internal qualities. Young boys whose fathers cook, nurture young children, attend ballet, volunteer in a soup kitchen or a nursing home, knit sweaters, or write poetry have a much broader range of options lifted up for them than do boys who see only a very restricted set of options as appropriate male behavior. Young girls whose mothers use tools, enjoy participating in sports, have a working knowledge about how an automobile runs, make decisions that relate to the whole family, clearly express their own needs, or discuss politics have that same wider range of options presented.

Of course, we cannot be sure that our own behavior will always have the impact that we desire on our children. Mary Beth and Michael are parents who are both extremely sensitive to sex-role stereotyping. Mary Beth had created for their three-year-old son, Peter, a small step-stool made of wood. Initially she found herself feeling good about giving her son at least to a small degree an alternative role model. Her good feelings were short-lived however, because she has heard Peter telling his friends on several different occasions that his father made the stool for him. The parents have concluded that any reality that doesn't quite fit into Peter's preconceived notions about what men and women do is rejected by him, at least temporarily. (So it's back to the tool box for Mary Beth!)

Language

David and Theresa were sitting at the kitchen table talking about "what I want to be when I grow up." David asked Theresa, "Do you want to be a fireman?" Theresa nodded vigorously. At this point I decided to enter the conversation, and said, "Now Theresa couldn't really be a fire*man*, could she? I think we should say fire*fighter*. That's a better word anyway because they do *fight* fires — and both men and women do the work." David looked at me with bemused puzzlement. Then he turned back to Theresa and said, "Theresa, do you want to be a *nurse* when you grow up?"

I suppose the moral is that parents should know when to stay out of their children's conversations, but this incident provided a humorous glimpse at a more serious problem: the in-built sexism in language.

Looking at our own language patterns, which means looking at the language that our children hear us use, is another way of examining our own behavior in terms of how it influences our child's attitudes and behavior. There have been some changes in recent years in commonly accepted language. Exclusive terminology has in some cases been eliminated from church readings, magazine articles, children's books, and other publications. But the terminology has persisted in a wide variety of written materials, TV shows, and, perhaps most importantly, in the way adults talk. By exclusive terminology we mean specifically male terms that are used to refer to all people: "man" to mean any person, "mankind" to mean all people, "policeman" to mean any police officer, "he" to mean any man or woman, boy or girl.

Young children do not make complex distinctions among various meanings of a word. They do not differentiate between "man" as referring to a real male person and "man" as referring to a generic person. Our inclusive language is important not only as a way of reflecting to children a worldview of sexual equality, but also as a way of modelling for them their own speech patterns, which in turn influence their thought patterns. The following excerpt from an article in the *Parenting for Peace and Justice Newsletter* illustrates that point with a junior-high-aged child. Sue, the mother, related this experience:

> School is in session again, and it only took two days this time to get me riled up about a sexist action by our 12-year-old daughter's English teacher. When assigning a poem topic, "What is a Teenager?" she suggested that the students use the pronoun "he" throughout the poem. The kids themselves protested, saying what about girl teenagers? But the teacher, a woman, insisted that "he" was a generic pronoun and could refer to both male and female gender.
>
> So after I read Jenny's poem, I remarked on the plethora of "he's" that started each line, and I also noted a particularly masculine definition and tone to the poem. I encouraged Jenny to change the poem to include the feminine pronoun, perhaps alternating "she" with "he," but as this was her first English assignment of the school year and the first assignment in the new and somewhat awesome "junior high," she was reluctant to go against what she perceived as an order by the teacher.[8]

There are many teachers who would have handled the situation differently, but the fact remains that there are significant adults in a child's life who do not model inclusive behavior through their language or, in this case, through specific directions about the children's language.

Humor

Another aspect of the language question relates to our jokes and other sources of humor. Recently I had a conversation with my sixteen-year-old son about the differences between the terms "girl," "woman," "dame," and "broad." Even though we would not have a similar discussion with our two- or three-year-olds, they can pick up the feeling behind certain terms, as well as the overall impression that someone is being trivialized by a remark. Very young children can understand what it means to be "made fun of."

New Information

Reading material and other sources of information provide adults
with a way not only to gain new information but also to keep
updated on current realities. Reading books and periodicals that
deal directly with sexism, with the effects of sexism (e.g., poverty
among women), as well as with the lives of women — famous and
not-so-famous — can expand our horizons. Music preformed by
feminist artists like Holly Near can also give us new perspectives.
Women's theater groups and women's art exhibits have the same
impact. A listing of some resources for adult reading and listening
can be found in the resource section.

Boy-Girl Incidents

One woman, an experienced early childhood educator, told me
that she feels that often adults who are dealing fairly effectively
with changing sex roles in their own lives are still not able to deal
effectively with similar changes in the ways they relate directly to
young children.

This teacher struggles in her own teaching to break down old
patterns in the ways she relates to the children, and she encourages
the other teachers on her staff to do the same. She will not say
things like, "All the boys get their coats. . . . Now all the girls get
their coats." She says that she catches herself falling back on those
distinctions but is working on new categorizations, for example,
"All the children with blue coats put yours on first today."

She feels that even seemingly neutral differentiations between
boys and girls can set an environment that does not discourage,
and perhaps encourages, sexist incidents among the children. As
parents, we do not usually have to make decisions about categoriz-
ing groups of children by sex except for situations like play groups
or parties. But, we often do deal with insults or taunts or practices
of exclusion based on sex. "Boys can't play here." "You throw like
a girl." "Sissy!" "No girls can come in here." It is important for
us to realize that children can indeed learn to operate in a different
way. They can learn to play and work together without setting up
sex-based barriers.

STRATEGIES WITH CHILDREN

Since very young children are so open to the world around them and especially to the ideas and influence of the people who love them, there is virtually no limit on the kinds of strategies that we can pursue with them. The only real limitation is our own creativity and energy. As with anything that implies or encourages change, however, we need to be gentle yet persistent with ourselves as well as with our children. Consider, then, the following suggestions.

Verbal Patterns and Associations

Besides the kind of exclusive language mentioned earlier, there are other language questions that relate to sex-role stereotypes and children. When our daughter, Theresa, was about two-and-a-half, I remember becoming aware that I was regularly commenting on her appearance. "Oh, Theresa, you look so pretty!" was often heard in our house, especially on Sunday mornings. Then, to add yet another level of unstated message, I would say, "Go show your daddy how pretty you look!"

I began to realize that I was not commenting in the same way on the boys' appearances. I felt that I was giving two messages to Theresa and to my sons. I was telling Theresa that her appearance was what really counted about her, and I was implying for all the children that the ultimate acceptance for a woman is the approval of a man.

What I finally decided was that while I really did not feel it was inappropriate to comment on a child's appearance, especially when it was something that they felt a great deal of pride about at the moment, I needed to make those comments equally to my sons and to my daughter.

So I worked at saying things like, "Your hair looks so nice. You did a good job of combing it," or "I really like that dress. That color is so pretty. It makes you look bright and shiny," or "That shirt looks nice on you. You look so dressed up." I also tried not to make a direct connection for Theresa between her appearance and a man's approval. Jim, of course, would often make his own comments about their appearances, which I felt was very different from my directing Theresa to Jim for his approval.

An experienced pre-school teacher reflected on the issue of children's appearance from a slightly different angle. Her thoughts offer a keen insight: "A level of sloppiness and not caring about one's appearance is considered very masculine. Here comes Billy and his shoes are untied and his coat is dragging, and we say, 'He's all boy!' I would say, 'No, he's dressing in a sloppy way. It has nothing to do with being a boy.'"

This same teacher, because of her concern about girls' often exaggerated preoccupation with clothes, says, "I've even gone so far as to decide not to comment at all on the girls' clothes. They will say to me, 'See my new sparkle sweatshirt,' and I will say, 'Yes, I see it,' and then get busy doing something else. I do acknowledge good play clothes and good play shoes. I'll say, 'Those shoes look like they'll be superfast shoes,' or 'You'll be able to climb well in those shoes.' I do this for both the boys and the girls."

In addition to words with regard to clothes and physical appearance, other words and word patterns are also related to basic attitudes and behaviors about sex roles. Consider the following words. To whom do we apply these descriptions — boys, girls, or both?

| cooperative | sweet | pretty | tough | active |
| assertive | strong | big | delicate | gentle |

We used to feel Theresa's arm muscles regularly and comment on how big her muscles were getting, just as we did with our sons. I said to Theresa as a baby and toddler, "My, what a big strong girl you are!" I have to confess that I didn't do as much to connect gentleness and other typical "feminine" characteristics with my boys. I did encourage them to be gentle with each other, with their friends, and with their toys, and I did encourage their efforts in more "delicate" pursuits like arts and crafts.

When the children were very young we decided on special family "love names" for each one of us. Jim became Honey Bear; Tom, Sugar Bear; Dave, Huggy Bear; and Theresa, Sweet Bear. When it came to deciding my name, the children immediately said, "Mama Bear." I laughed and told them that "Mama" was my role in the family and I was very happy about being the "mama"; however, I wanted another love name just like everybody else. (I stand before you as Happy Bear.)

Feedback on Feelings

One of the most telling effects of a sexist society on the lives of men is the difficulty many men have in expressing their feelings. This reality has endangered marriages, prevented deep friendships from developing between men, made intimacy of any kind more difficult for them to maintain, contributed to anxiety-related health problems, and often been part of the reason for a man's violent behavior in the home.

As parents, anything that we do to encourage children to clarify and express their feelings will facilitate their growth as complete human beings, men and women, as well as improve their ability to communicate effectively. A simple acknowledging of an obvious display of feeling — "You are really happy when Mommy comes home, aren't you?" or, "I know you feel sad and kind of empty inside because your friend is moving away," or "I think you're feeling angry because someone wrote on your picture" — is important to a child because it implicitly says that those feelings are okay. It is particularly important for young girls to know that there are appropriate times for them to be angry, since adult women often find it difficult to be assertive about expressing anger.

Reading

In *Little Women* Mother March gives this advice to Jo: "To be loved and chosen by a good man is the best and sweetest thing which can happen to a woman. Prepare for it, so when the happy day comes, you may feel ready for the duties and worthy of the joy."[9] Messages in children's books in the 1980s may not be stated quite this directly, but unfortunately sexism is still a reality in children's literature. Since as parents we are very much involved in the selection of books for our pre-schoolers, criteria for this selection can be helpful:

• Check the visuals.
   − Are females pictured as often as males?
   − Are females pictured in roles secondary to males — waiting on them. learning from them, being protected by them, following behind? Are there the same number of pictures of males in subordinate roles vis-à-vis women?

  – Are women pictured in trivial or ridiculous ways?
  – How many pictures show females in an active role? A passive role?
  – How many of the visuals show females in a way that emphasizes appearances?
  – Are men pictured taking care of children? Showing emotion?

• Check the language.

  – Is generic male terminology used (for example, indefinite "he" for either sex)?
  – In young children's books, are the animals male or female?
  – Are words used that are demeaning to women (for example, "broad," "girls" used for grown women, "nag," "shrew," etc.)?

• Check the lifestyles.

  – Are women seen in a wide variety of lifestyles, or as confined to certain ones?
  – Are two-parent families seen as "healthy families" and variations seen as "problems"?

• Check the heroes.

  – Are women shown in positions of authority?
  – Are women shown who have worked and are working for women's rights and for social change in other areas (for example, Sojourner Truth, Susan B. Anthony, Rosa Parks, Jane Addams)?

• Look at the relationships among people.

  – Do the females function mainly in roles that put them in a position of dependency on males?
  – Are men and women shown as being mutually supportive of each other?

• Consider institutional sexism.

  – Is there any indication in the book of the problems women face in our society?

> – Is there any indication that solutions to injustice toward women demand more than individual good will — that structures must change?

- Check the author or editor.
  > – How many of our children's books are written, edited, or illustrated by a woman?
  >
  > – Is there an indication in the biographical data that the author has any concerns about sexism or sex-role stereotyping?[10]

The resource section on pp. 119-120 contains a bibliography for young readers that is especially good in terms of the following:

- Men and women, boys and girls shown in activities often considered "untypical" for their sex (labelled A).
- Women shown as achievers and in positions of authority (labelled B).
- People shown actively working against sexism (labelled C).

Toys and Play

Very few parents need to be told how important play is in the life of their pre-schooler. It is the child's whole day, aside from sleeping and eating. Play is the way children solve problems, build strength, learn about social norms like sharing and cooperating, develop gross and fine motor skills, express imagination, and build self-esteem and respect for others. As parents and other adult nurturers we give our children messages about our own attitudes toward sex roles by the toys we give them as well as by the kinds of play and other interests that we encourage for them.

Toys, which are in many respects the tools of childhood, should give children an ever-wider view of the world and of their own competence in dealing with that world. Yet the toy shelves in stores today give very different messages to children. Unfortunately, an extremely high percentage of toys have nothing to do with problem-solving, competency, skill-building, or nurturing. In chapter 5 we will examine the level of violence in toys for young children. In terms of sex-role stereotyping, that concern is important because the toys of violence are aimed specifically at young boys. The message is very clear: to be a man you must control other people. Guns and other weapons are the way that you maintain that control. You don't have to deal with differing points of view if you have a submachine gun in your hands.

Letty Cottin Pogrebin in her book *Growing Up Free: Raising Your Child in the 80s* carries that concern one step farther when she applies it to grown men: "Because man perceives himself to be the legitimate power wielder, the tools of power belong to him whether he keeps them well oiled in a gun rack over his mantle, or 'keeps' them only symbolically in the form of toy guns given to male children."[11]

The sexism inherent in toys for young girls is different. There the message has nothing to do with power (except for "She-Ra, the Princess of Power"), and very little to do with competence, except in the domestic area. Little girls' toys are filled with images of the importance of high fashion, from plastic high-heeled shoes to "Beverly Hills Bath Boutique," to the Rich and Famous Dolls, to a thirty-piece play make-up set, to toy jump ropes and exercise sets labelled "Get in Shape, Girl." Even though the exercise gear is aimed at a slightly older child, the over-all impression from all of these toys is very clear: the most important skill for a young girl to achieve is maintaining her appearance.

There is still of course a range of toys that deals with everyday household chores — vacuums, sewing sets, laundry items, grocery shopping carts, irons, kitchen sets, dishes, etc. Unfortunately, these toys show only girls on the package. As far as the toy manufacturers are concerned, household items are "For Girls Only."

Dolls, of course, are available in great numbers, and in some variety of style, even though they are still almost all white. I do have questions about the adult, svelte figures with the long silky hair. I watched a four-year-old girl spend a half-hour combing the hair of one of these dolls; then she put her into the arms of the boy doll to be carried around — as a "pretty princess."

Given these realities in the world of toy manufacturing and advertising, what are some practical strategies for parents?

- Encourage both boys and girls to play with the kinds of toys that contribute to the skills and values you cherish as adults, e.g., dolls, puzzles, blocks, stuffed animals, building sets of all kinds, balls.

- Let children see the adults in their lives modelling "atypical" behavior. We were at a party recently with several other families, and at one point I became very aware of the kind of behavior we were modelling for the children. Two of the families had little babies. As soon as those families arrived, their babies were eagerly taken and held and bounced on the laps of other women in the group. During the whole afternoon that we were together, except for when they were with their own fathers, the babies were always being held by the women or by the older girls in the group, in fact most often by these girls. This is a group of "liberated" people, but old patterns die hard.

  Another way of creating "new patterns" is to show children that women enjoy playing with trains, building environments for the train, playing with balls, or sledding. Similarly, men enjoy playing with dolls, going to tea parties, making potholders on looms, or painting.

- Encourage children to pursue interests and activities that are truly their own. In order to know what these interests are, young children have to be exposed to a myriad of possibilities — crayons and paints, needles and yarn, cutting and pasting, athletics, tricycles, wagons, hammers and nails, dance and dramatic play, musical instruments. This will begin to give them some feel for whether or not they want to take ballet lessons, play soccer, learn needlepoint, build things from wood, play the clarinet, etc.

  One experienced early childhood educator sets up play areas in her classroom with many possibilities that she finds attractive for both boys and girls — for example, a restaurant, a toy store (complete with a cash register), a bank, environments for animals (she doesn't like to think in terms of zoos and cages).

- Pre-school girls spend 75 percent of their time playing house; boys spend about 30 percent.[12] Watch your children play house. Who assumes which roles? Do you need to intervene to encourage a boy to play the Mommy or a girl the Daddy? Or at least to raise a question about how the roles are decided?

Celebrations of Women

Both boys and girls need to see women as achievers, as people
who have made and continue to make significant contributions to
the betterment of humankind. Unfortunately, women's lives and
accomplishments are celebrated very rarely in our culture. So it is
up to us as parents to make those celebrations a part of our family
traditions. The following is a list of "Birthdays of Notable Women"
adapted from a list in *Equal Their Chances* by June Shapiro, Sylvia
Kramer, and Catherine Hunnerberg:[13]

Lucretia Mott	January 3
Joan of Arc	January 6
Corazon Aquino	January 25
Elizabeth Blackwell	February 3
Rosa Parks	February 4
Susan B. Anthony	February 15
Harriet Tubman	March 10*
Mother Jones	May 1
Rachel Carson	May 27
Mary McLeod Bethune	June 10
Helen Keller	June 27
Amelia Earhart	July 24
Eleanor Roosevelt	October 11
Dorothy Day	November 8
Elizabeth C. Stanton	November 12
Sarah Grimke	November 26

If we chose even one or two of these women each year and had a
"birthday party," complete with time to talk about the woman,
that would be a significant beginning.

The Work People Do

We were visiting the home of some good friends who had a Chicano
woman employed in their home to do cleaning and some cooking.
As both our families were finishing our breakfast, I began to feel
very uncomfortable. Maria, who had served the meal, was now
beginning to clean the dishes. I was in a near panic about what

---

*Death date; birth unknown.

our young children would internalize from the experience about Chicano people, about who serves whom, and about the work that women of color do. I urged the children to clear their own dishes in what I hope was a nonchalant manner, but I'm sure they sensed an element of the frantic in my words.

I made a point of talking with Maria during the day and asking about her own family — actually a limited English-Spanish dialogue. I also talked to our children about Maria's work, about how difficult it is to take care of someone else's home and then go to your own home to do the same work. That experience has stayed with me, even though it occurred years ago, as a reminder of the necessity of helping young children value and respect the work of all people.

I think this has particular relevance when considering the work of women, since society in general devalues the work that all women do, particularly women of color. Whatever we do with our very young children to begin developing in them positive attitudes toward the work that people do will have ramifications in their attitudes toward all women, toward all people of color, and toward people who are economically poor. In "Teaching Pre-Schoolers About Work — A Complex Task," an article in the *Bulletin* of the Council on Interracial Books for Children, Geraldine Wilson, an early childhood specialist, presents several key concepts that are important guidelines for parents also:

- Work is what people do when they are not playing.
- Work is what mothers or fathers do when they clean house and take care of children.
- Some jobs are outside (farmers, meter readers, construction workers); some jobs are indoors (secretaries, computer operators, disc jockeys); some jobs are underground, under water, in the air.
- Some work is dangerous, like washing windows on the outside of high buildings.
- Some work makes you very tired, like bending over to pick string beans for a long time every day.
- When people go to a job, they get money in return for the work they do.
- Some people make lots and lots of money for their work;

others, who work just as hard, make very little money.

- Parents and family members who take care of children, do housework, and cook do not get paid as if they were on a job. They do the work because it is important, it needs to be done, and they agree to do it.

- There is a spirit, a feeling inside many people, that makes them want to work hard at something, even if they do not make money. Some people like the work they do even if they do not get enough money.

- People sometimes work for no money because they want to help other people. They might help sick people in a hospital, inmates in a prison, visitors to a museum, children and teachers in a school.

- People often do very important work without earning very much (artists, jazz musicians, day-care and Head Start staff, coal miners).[14]

Many of these concepts and attitudes are encouraged in children through everyday conversation. Visits to the library, grocery store, art museum, or park, rides on a bus, or just a walk down the street provide us with opportunities. "Look how fast that woman's fingers fly over the keys on the register!" "You have to be a very careful driver to be able to drive one of those trucks!" "That man must get tired and dirty holding that jackhammer for a long time." "Look how clean he makes these floors!"

The work of the homemaker needs to be included in this discussion. The Multicultural Project for Communication and Education in Cambridge, Mass., suggests several very imaginative ways for educators to help children develop a healthy respect for work done within the family. The one described below could be adapted for use by parents.

Wall Display or Notebook: Compare the jobs done by a homemaker to similar work outside the home. Children who have been to hospitals or visited clinics could describe similarities and differences between health care work done by their parents, when children are hurt or sick, and the health care work of nurses and doctors. The work of preparing or serving foods for a restaurant can be compared with the work of preparing meals for a family. Children may be asked to compare child care in the home with the way child care work is organized in the day care center. Make a chart, or describe the comparisons in a notebook, organized according to type of work. Continue adding to it after community trips or visits from members of the community. If parents, whose paid work is related to services, are able to describe their work to the children, ask them to help the children notice the similarities and differences to work in the home. (Some other services include sewing clothes, laundry work, furniture repair, and aspects of clerical work).

Discuss the cost of providing services in and out of the home so that children begin to appreciate the enormous effort and variety of work that is done in the home for no pay.[15]

Critical Viewing of TV and Advertisements

The following guidelines are offered as a prod to our own "critical thinking and viewing skills" as well as idea starters for discussions with young children:

- How many women have major TV roles? minor roles? Perhaps the family could log its TV watching for a week somewhat as follows:

Name of Show	Number of Major Male Characters	Number of Major Female Characters	Number of Minor Male Characters	Number of Minor Female Characters

(Note: Include *Sesame Street* in your log of TV watching. Ask the children especially about the major muppet characters — Big Bird, Ernie, Bert, Grover, Count, Oscar, and Cookie Monster. Do they realize that they are all male? What do they think about that?)

- Treatment of sex and woman's body:
    - What percentage of women in the shows we watch is exceptionally attractive physically? How does this compare to the percentage of men?
    - How often are the women characters attired in a sexually provocative way (e.g., in *Mike Hammer, Miami*

Vice, etc.)? Often pre-schoolers don't see these shows; but they may see them advertised.

  − In how many commercials is a woman's body used as decoration? Note especially perfume commercials.

• What personal qualities reflected through characterizations on TV are shown primarily in one sex? For example, Leadership: male or female? Compassion: male or female? Clear thinking in emergencies: male or female?

• Are women seen primarily as dependent on men, or as capable of directing their own lives?

• List the occupational roles of men and women as depicted in the shows we see in a week.

• How often does a man use violence to solve a conflict?

• Do any of the shows make an attempt to deal with injustice toward women? With changing sex roles?

• How many times are women made to appear incapable, or intellectually inferior to men?

• How many times does a man solve a problem for a woman? How many times does a woman solve a problem for a man?

• How many times are men evaluated according to

  − the amount of money they have or flaunt?

  − the prestige of their occupation?

  − how "tough" they are?

The kinds of stereotypes that are reinforced for adults and for children through TV and other media such as magazines and movies need to be countered. This countering can be done by us as parents in several ways, for instance,

• by helping the children become critical of what they see and read; by using the sexism against itself; even by saying things like, "Why do you think they have that woman in that picture?"

• by talking about the sexism in TV programming.

• by encouraging the children to read stories and watch TV shows that provide role models opposed to prevalent sex-role stereotypes — e.g., the *Cosby Show,* or a TV special on a woman's life.[16]

No one of these strategies will change the pervasive nature of sexism and sex-role stereotyping in our lives; yet any one can be a beginning for a different way of thinking and behaving in one family, and therefore in many families.

Notes

1. From the poem by Judy Chicago, "Merger: A Vision of the Future."
2. Council on Interracial Books for Children, *Stereotypes, Distortions, and Omissions in U.S. History Textbooks* (New York: Racism and Sexism Resource Center for Educators, 1977), p. 131.
3. Council on Interracial Books for Children, *Human and Anti-Human Values in Children's Books* (New York: Racism and Sexism Resource Center for Educators, 1976), p. 11.
4. Project Beginning Equal, *Beginning Equal: A Manual about Nonsexist Child-rearing for Infants and Toddlers* (New York: Women's Action Alliance and the Pre-School Association, Inc., 1983), p. 9.
5. Alice Sterling Honig, "Research in Review: Sex Role Socialization in Early Childhood," *Young Children*, vol. 38, no. 6, September 1983, p. 58.
6. Letty Cottin Pogrebin, *Growing Up Free: Raising Your Child in the 80s* (New York: McGraw-Hill, 1980), p. 357.
7. James and Kathleen McGinnis, *Christian Parenting for Peace and Justice* (Nashville: Discipleship Resources, 1981), p. 60.
8. Sue Williams, "What's a Mother to Do?" *Parenting for Peace and Justice Newsletter*, no. 23, October 1986, p. 1.
9. As quoted in "Identifying Sexism in Children's Books," script for sound filmstrip (New York: Council on Interracial Books for Children, 1978).
10. Kathleen and James McGinnis, *Parenting for Peace and Justice* (Maryknoll, N.Y.: Orbis, 1981), pp. 87–88.
11. Pogrebin, *Growing Up Free*, p. 377.
12. Ibid., p. 353.
13. June Shapiro, Sylvia Kramer, and Catherine Hunnerberg, *Equal Their Chances: Children's Activities for Non-Sexist Learning* (Englewood Cliffs, N.J.: Prentice-Hall, Inc., 1981), p. 151.
14. "Teaching Pre-Schoolers About Work—A Complex Task," *Bulletin*, Council on Interracial Books for Children, vol. 16, no. 4, p. 12.
15. Jessie Wenning and Sheli Wortis, *Made by Human Hands: A Curriculum for Teaching Young Children about Work and Working People* (Cambridge, Mass.: The Multicultural Project for Communication and Education, 1985), pp. 16–17.
16. Adapted from McGinnis, *Parenting for Peace and Justice*, pp. 86–87.

Chapter 4

Respect for All: Older People and People with Disabilities

"Label Jars...Not People"[1]

Adam, a lively five-year-old, entered the nursing home with his family. Immediately he said, "Yuck, it smells. I *knew* it was going to smell!" When his dad asked him what he meant, Adam's reply was revealing: "My friends, Ken and Joe, have been to a nursing home before. They told me it would smell. They said all old people smell terrible!"

Pre-schoolers and older people are often seen as natural allies. The bubbling enthusiasm of the very young is very attractive to older people, and the wisdom, warmth, and availability of the elders is definitely a bonus for young children. A similar kind of alliance can be found between young children and people with disabilities — young and old. Pre-schoolers have the capacity to see through external differences in a person and recognize the core — who the person really is. Even though they know someone is in a wheelchair, or walks with braces, or cannot hear, they *can* realize that those aspects are not the entire person.

I stress *can*, because at times young children do not relate openly and lovingly with people with disabilities or with older people. One reason for this is that society implants, even in young minds, inaccurate images of older people and of people with disabilities. Ageism and handicapism are both all too prevalent in our culture, and they mean not only inaccurate and stereotypical thinking, but also unequal and discriminatory treatment.

Ageism is any attitude, action, or institutional structure that subordinates a person or group because of age *or* any assignment of roles in society on the basis of age. Ageism is usually practiced against older people, but it is also practiced against the young. Ageism can be individual, cultural, or institutional, and it can be intentional or unintentional. The following are examples: *Individual:* "She's too old to wear jeans"; "My grandfather is too old to understand me." *Cultural:* "You can't teach an old dog new tricks"; "There's no fool like an old fool." *Institutional:* compulsory retirement; the expectation that older people will be volunteers rather than paid employees.

Results of ageism in our culture include:

- Ageism makes it easier to ignore the frequently oppressive social and economical situation of older people in U.S. society.

- Ageism permits employers to retire higher-paid older workers with seniority and to replace them with lower-paid younger workers.

- Ageism protects younger people from thinking about things they fear (aging, illness, death).

- Ageism sabotages the self-image of older people and is an attack on their dignity as human beings.[2]

"Handicapism" refers to stereotyping, prejudice, and discrimination practiced by society against disabled people.[3] Terminology referring to people with disabilities is very important. Words can reinforce stereotypes and negative ideas, or they can be allies in building more positive attitudes. Below in the left column is a listing of terms considered by many people active in the disability rights movement to be offensive; in the right column are the preferred terms.

Offensive	**Preferred**
Handicap, handicapped person	Disability, disabled person
Deaf and dumb, deaf-mute, the deaf	Deaf, hearing disability, hearing impairment
Mongoloid	Down's Syndrome

Cripple, crippled	Orthopedic disability, mobility impaired, disabled person
The blind	Blind person, sight disability, visually impaired
Retard, retardate, idiot, imbecile, feeble-minded	Retarded, mental impairment, mentally disabled
Crazy, maniac, insane, mentally ill	Emotional disability, emotional impairment, developmentally disabled

The Minnesota 1976 Governors Conference on Handicapped Individuals proposed that the following categories be deleted from library cataloging systems: abnormal children; abnormalities, human; atypical children; backward; children, retarded; children, feeble-minded.[4]

There are, or course, economic results of handicapism. According to a Louis Harris Survey, 66.7 percent of disabled people between the ages of sixteen and sixty-four are unemployed. Figures are much higher for certain kinds of disabilities.[5] For every dollar earned by a non-disabled white male, comparably qualified disabled people earn the following:

Disabled white male	60 cents
Disabled white female	24 cents
Disabled Black male	25 cents
Disabled Black female	12 cents[6]

The strategies we suggest aim at the following:

- increasing our own knowledge and understanding about the economic and social realities of aging in this country and those same realities for people with disabilities
- laying the foundation for critical thinking skills with regard to cultural messages about older people and people with disabilities
- building positive attitudes toward the disabled and the elderly
- building self-esteem for disabled children

ADULT STRATEGIES

Informing Ourselves

Reading and contact with people who have disabilities and with older people are two primary methods for increasing our own level of understanding. There are disability rights activists in many communities — those people who are actively engaged in the struggle to overcome stereotypic attitudes, to change unjust policies and practices, and to advocate realistic independent living opportunities for disabled people. It is a civil rights movement that has gained momentum in the last ten to fifteen years. If there are such organizations in your community, contact them, get on their mailing lists, perhaps even volunteer at their offices.

Some of us live with disabled people in our immediate families, our extended families, our neighborhoods, and our churches. The personal contact already exists in our lives and probably in the lives of our children. Others of us need to be conscious of making those contacts. That is where the disability rights and independent living groups can be a help. Jim Tuscher is an activist and a member of the staff of Paraquad, an independent living organization in St. Louis. His comments about personal contact among children have bearing on its importance for adults as well. "The attitude thing is simply a question of contact," Tuscher says. "When you shut disabled people off in a womb-like environment like special schools, two things happen. The disabled person gets the message that he can't make it in the real world. And a parallel attitude is being developed in the other kids — that kid is so different they have to haul him off, he can't be with us. What's gonna happen twenty-five years later when that able-bodied kid is a director of personnel and a guy comes in a wheelchair for a job?"[7]

Reading about the lives of people with disabilities, e.g., Franklin Roosevelt, Itzhak Perlman, Helen Keller, or Alicia Alonso, is another way — obviously second-best — to "come into contact" with the disabled. You can subscribe to a periodical from a disability rights or independent living group.[8] Or you can read books like *The Unexpected Minority: Handicapped Children in America* by John Gliedman and William Roth (Harcourt, Brace, Jovanovich, 1980), the first comprehensive study to apply a civil rights lens to the problems of both disabled children and adults, or *Parenting*

Your Disabled Child by Bernard Ikeler (Westminster, 1986), tested advice for parents about ways to facilitate the growth of disabled children toward rich and productive lives. The same suggestions about personal contact and reading apply to informing ourselves about older people. All of us have contact with older people in our families, neighborhoods, and churches. The question really becomes one of the quality of that contact. Do we allow ourselves time to really be with the older people we know? Do we share with them what's going on in our lives, and are we genuinely interested in what's going on in theirs? Do we seek their advice and ask their opinions? Do we draw from their wealth of experience to enrich our own lives and those of our children? I have often found myself saying to our children, "Let's ask Grandpa about that!" whenever a question about farming comes up, e.g., What does it mean to shuck corn? What kind of work did horses do on the farm? Is it hard to milk cows? How do the eggs come out of the chicken? Unfortunately we often did not get around to asking Grandpa when we saw him the next time, and I regret the richness that we've missed.

Our personal contacts may be marred by misperceptions and stereotypes that we have about older people. One quick way simply to check the accuracy of our own ideas is to take the following "Facts on Aging Quiz." Correct answers can be found in the endnote on p. 73.

FACTS ON AGING QUIZ

T F   1. The majority of old people (past age sixty-five) are senile (i.e., defective in memory, disoriented, or demented).

T F   2. All five senses tend to decline in old age.

T F   3. Most old people have no interest in, or capacity for, sexual relations.

T F   4. Lung capacity tends to decline in old age.

T F   5. The majority of old people feel miserable most of the time.

T F   6. Aged drivers have fewer accidents per person than drivers under age sixty-five.

T F   7. Most older workers are not able to work as effectively as younger workers.

T F   8. About 80 percent of the aged are healthy enough to carry out their normal activities.

T F   9. Most old people are set in their ways and unable to change.

T F   10. It is almost impossible for most old people to learn new things.

T F   11. Most old people are pretty much alike.

T F   12. The majority of old people are seldom bored.

T F   13. The majority of old people are socially isolated and lonely.

T F   14. Over 25 percent of the U.S. population are now age sixty-five or over.

T F   15. The majority of old people are working or would like to have some kind of work to do (including housework and volunteer work).[9]

Reading about the realities of life for our elders can be a way to expand our own horizons and counter any misperceptions that we have. Some recommended books are listed in the resource pages. In addition, it is particularly enlightening to be on the mailing lists for groups like the Gray Panthers, 3635 Chestnut Street, Philadelphia, PA 19104, or the American Association of Retired Persons (AARP), 1901 K Street, N.W., Washington, DC 20006. Most communities and many churches have a Task Force on Aging or a Council on Aging. Any of these groups are resources for continually updated information. The Gray Panthers deserve specific mention because of their long struggle to combat discrimination against the elderly. The following words of Maggie Kuhn are typical of their philosophy:

> Our decade is witnessing the rise of a very different generation of elders. We live longer. We're better educated and more articulate. And we are becoming aware how our society puts us down. I would hope that the revolution of the elders...would be a unifying force in a society that is fear-ridden and divided. Age is the great universalizer.... The Gray Panthers and other recommended groups are muscling in on society. We'll do it with militancy, demonstrations, anything to get a place at the table.[10]

One last source of reading is biographies of people who in the advanced years of their lives have made outstanding contributions in a number of fields, people like Pablo Picasso, W. E. B. Du Bois, Golda Meir, Frederick Douglass, Grandma Moses, Maria Montoya, Ben Franklin.

Humor

"Mommy, look at me, I'm blind," says pre-school Carol as she bumps into a wall and falls down with a dramatic flourish. That is a young child's attempt at humor, unknowingly at the expense of someone else.

How often, though, are our own sources of humor derived from the perceived differences between ourselves and the disabled or the elderly? Senility, often inaccurately considered synonymous with old age, loss of physical beauty, lack of productive capabilities, inflexibility, and complete loss of sexual feelings, is often used as the basis for jokes about older people. In a similar vein, people with disabilities have to contend with humor based on qualities others attribute to them. These attributes are often connected to their specific disability (especially mental impairments of any kind), or to an inaccurate connection of disabilities (e.g., jokes that imply that people in wheelchairs are retarded), or to other general misperceptions about the disabled (e.g., asexuality, inability to take charge of one's own life, inability to assume any kind of leadership role).

When young children hear us using old age or disability as the basis for humor, they are bound to think of the elderly or the disabled as less important, less powerful, and less worthy of their esteem.

STRATEGIES WITH CHILDREN

Our children have just seen the movie *Mask*, which chronicles the life of a boy with a disease resulting in severe facial disfigurement. The film is flawed in its presentation of the life of a disabled person and has been critiqued for that by disability rights people. For our young teens, however, viewing the film presented them with an opportunity to expand their own sensitivities and to be angry at the barriers society places in the way of a person with disabilities. We had some good conversation about what it means to be different, how important it is to believe in yourself, and what a difference it makes for anyone to have the support of others who really care about you.

This kind of a film is not appropriate for pre-schoolers, but there are other opportunities, including those we create ourselves, that can aid our young children in growing in respect for people with disabilities and for older people.

Association with People

Young children need opportunities to be with older people and people with disabilities in all kinds of everyday activities as well as structured learning situations. Many of us have warm thoughts about times spent with grandparents or greatgrandparents; they left an indelible mark on our memory because of some incident or ritual or place that was really rather ordinary but became extraordinary to us. My husband, Jim, remembers his grandmother's feather bed, a warm quilt, and the San Francisco fog horn. My own children often talk about the special way their grandmother makes fried eggs. They'll ask about "that funny man, the one who makes us laugh" — an uncle of mine whom they've seen only a few times in their lives.

Making time for these kinds of relationships to grow, whether among family or special friends, is vital not only to a child's individual development, but also to his or her attitudes toward older people in general. There are also times when planned contacts with older people are important: visits to senior citizens centers, time spent with older people in a retirement community or a nursing home, all of these, of course, with some preparation and definitely with supervision.

Foster Grandparent programs are available in some communities, where low-income older adults have the opportunity to provide individualized attention to children with special needs. The program is a part of ACTION, and information can be obtained from a toll-free ACTION number: (800) 424-8580.

Sometimes there are ordinary, everyday relationships with disabled people that are possible for our children. At other times we need to create those situations. It is important for non-disabled children to interact with disabled children — at a "Y" program, a church event, activities around a Special Olympics, programs sponsored by advocacy and service groups, perhaps something at a school for children with a specific disability.

It is also important for both disabled and non-disabled children to have role models of disabled adults who are active participants in society. Early childhood education programs can include classroom visits to disabled persons. Some of the same kinds of groups and programs mentioned above are good sources for adult resource people. It is a good learning opportunity for a child to visit a disabled person at his or her place of work, to actually see the contribution of that person. Even though pre-schoolers will often not understand the work, they will begin to form an image of people with disabilities at work.

Visual Representations

Since very young children tend to be literal as well as visual, it is important for them to see pictures and posters of older people and people with disabilities. We can't have pictures on our walls that represent every different kind of situation, but we can put pictures on our refrigerator or on a bulletin board and tell our children that these are pictures that we like.

There are several sources for pictures of disabled people. A photo package, "Resource Photos for Mainstreaming," is available for purchase from the Women's Action Alliance, Inc., 370 Lexington Ave., New York, NY 10017. You can also clip pictures from periodicals such as "Exceptional Parent" (296 Boylston St., Boston, MA 02116) and "Ability" (P.O. Box 5311, Mission Hills, CA 91345).

Most families have pictures of older people more readily available, but the American Association of Retired Persons (AARP), 1909 K St., N.W., Washington, DC 20006, is a good resource if you're looking for more materials.

Puppets are another good learning tool and visual opportunity for children with regard to both the disabled and the elderly. Puppets can be handmade. One distributor (Sign Language Shoppe, Box 377, East Islip, NY 11730) has fabric puppets of animals with various disabilities. An outstanding puppet program that a preschool or church may want to consider is "Kids on the Block," 1712 Eye St., N.W., Suite 1008, Washington, DC 20006.

Critical Reading and Viewing

Children's literature can help us as parents to develop positive attitudes toward older people and people with disabilities. TV can
also be a source of positive learning. Unfortunately, both ageism
and handicapism have invaded the world of children's books and
children's TV programming. The resource list at the end of the
book suggests some books for children, books that foster respect
and sensitivity toward people with disabilities. The *Bulletin* of
the Council on Interracial Books for Children is a good source for
keeping updated on new children's books. The American Association of Retired Persons (AARP) has had a Book Purchase Project
since 1977; it provides names of books dealing specifically with
older people.

It is also important to sharpen our critical reading and viewing skills and share some of these (where appropriate) with our
young children. The following criteria were developed by the Gray
Panther Media Watch National Committee:

- *Stereotypes:* Any over-simplification or generalization of the
  characteristics and language of old age that demeans or rid-
  icules older people. Examples:
    - *Appearance:* face always blank or expressionless; body
      always bent over and infirm.
    - *Clothing:* men's baggy and unpressed; women's frumpy
      and ill-fitting.
    - *Speech:* halting and high-pitched.
    - *Personality:* stubborn, rigid, forgetful.

  In comparison to others, are older people depicted as less
  capable? Do they have less to contribute? Are their ideas
  usually old-fashioned? Is the "rocking-chair" image predom-
  inant?

- *Distortions:* The use of myth or outright falsehoods to depict old age as either an idyllic or moribund stage of life.
  Examples:
    - Are older people depicted as intruders or meddlers in
      the relationships of others?
    - Are older people ridiculed when they show sexual feel-
      ings?

- When there is an age difference in romantic relationships, are older women accorded the same respect as older men?
- Are old people patronized and treated as children?

• *Omissions:* The exclusions or avoidance of older people, of their life concerns, and of the positive aspects of aging. Examples:

- Are the oppressive conditions under which older people must live in society analyzed? Are alternatives to the existing conditions presented?
- In any discussion of social and economic issues, are the perspectives of older people included?
- Are older people directly involved in writing, directing, and producing the program?
- How about the acting? Are there valid reasons for young actors to play the roles of older people?[11]

Many of the Media Watch criteria can be applied directly to children's books. The following questions could be asked about children's books:

• *Stereotypes*

- Are older women presented as "crones" or witches or sources of evil?
- Are older people always presented as having physical disabilities?
- Is senility portrayed as synonymous with old age?[12]

• *Characterization*

- Is there character development of the older people in the story?
- Would children reading the story regard the older characters as interesting people?
- Are the older characters shown as active, inventive, and quick-thinking, or are they cast mainly in passive, supportive roles?

• *Omissions:* Are older characters present in the stories at all?

The kind of critical viewing and reading that is called for with regard to the disabled can be aided by the following guidelines:

- Are disabled people portrayed as objects of pity?
- Are disabled people seen as victims of violence? There is some reality to this depiction, but when disabled people are constantly portrayed in this way, there is a reinforcement of an image of them as completely helpless. (An example is the film *Wait Until Dark,* about a blind woman terrorized by a gang.)
- Does an evil aura surround the disabled character? The profusion of disabled villains in children's literature as well as in media portrayals adds to an immediate connection between disability and wickedness, e.g., Rumpelstiltskin, Dr. Strangelove.
- Is the "Super Crip" syndrome present? Does the disabled character display exceptional, almost superhuman qualities that enable him or her to function well, e.g., the TV character "Ironside"?
- Are disabled people used as the source of humorous remarks or incidents, e.g., Mr. Magoo?
- Is the disabled person blamed for his or her condition? In other words, is the impression given that through sheer self-determination the person will be able to "overcome," ignoring the very real institutional barriers that society presents? Examples are to be found on many TV medical shows.
- Is the disabled person viewed as non-sexual? Does the portrayal eliminate the possibility of genuine loving relationships for disabled people?
- Are disabled people shown as incapable of full participation in everyday life? This is mainly a question of omission — a complete lack of disabled characters functioning in a creative, positive way on a day-to-day basis.[13]

While certainly no one of these strategies will change the institutional nature of ageism or handicapism in the larger society, any one of them can begin a journey for very young minds that will eventually lead them to question assumptions, to challenge practices, and to work for a society where *all* people are respected, appreciated, and treated in an equitable manner.

Notes

1. Logo of the Human Policy Press, Syracuse, N.Y.

2. *Bulletin,* Council on Interracial Books for Children, vol. 7, no. 6, 1976, p. 11.

3. In this chapter we will use the terms "disabled people," "people with disabilities," and "the disabled" interchangeably for stylistic reasons. We do acknowledge that "people with disabilities" is definitely the preferable term, because it signifies that people are more than their disabilities.

4. *Bulletin,* vol. 8, nos. 6 and 7, 1977, p. 5.

5. *ICD Survey of Disabled Americans: Bringing Disabled Americans into the Mainstream,* conducted for the International Center for the Disabled by Louis Harris and Associates, Inc., March 1986.

6. From Disability Rights Education and Defense Fund, Inc., in James McGinnis, *Educating for Peace and Justice,* vol. 1: *National Dimensions* (St. Louis: Institute for Peace and Justice, 1985), p. 186.

7. Judy J. Newmark, "Disabled Americans: A Question of Rights," *St. Louis Post-Dispatch, PD Magazine,* January 29, 1984, p. 6.

8. Several sources for regular updated information:

- Mainstream, Inc., 1200 15th St., N.W., Washington, DC 20005.

- PACER Center (Parent Advocacy Coalition for Educational Rights), 4704 Chicago Ave., South, Minneapolis, MN 55401.

- Center for Independence of the Disabled of New York City (CIDNY), 853 Broadway, New York, NY 10003.

9. "Facts on Aging Quiz" (adapted from E. Palmore, "Facts on Aging: A Short Quiz." *Gerontologist,* 17, 1977, pp. 315–320). Correct answers: True: nos. 2, 4, 6, 8, 12, 15; False: nos. 1, 3, 5, 7, 9, 10, 11, 13, 14. The correct percentage for no. 14 is 11.5 percent, a 1983 figure, according to the Congressional Office of Technology Assessment.

10. Margaret Kuhn quoted in *Everybody's Studying Us,* commentaries by Irene Paull and cartoons by Bulbul. Volcano Press, Inc., 330 Ellis St., San Francisco, CA 94102, 1976, p. 64.

11. James McGinnis, *Educating for Peace and Justice,* vol. 1: *National Dimensions,* p. 169.

12. Ibid., p. 170

13. *Bulletin,* vol. 8, nos. 6 and 7, 1977, pp. 4–9.

Chapter 5

Violence and Peace: Here and Around the World

"Blessed are the peacemakers. They shall be called the children of God" (Matthew 5).

Yesterday my two-and-a-half-year-old son, Klaas, suddenly hit the floor, spread-eagled on his stomach, and announced, "When the bombs come and the buildings crash down, you have to go like this." He and Janna (age four) have been fascinated and moved by the pictures of the Israeli invasion of Lebanon they have seen in the newspaper. I've answered their questions concretely, with the information they have asked for. I've tried to keep the answers to "why" questions short, simple, and honest, but that's hard. I find myself avoiding any response to their own situation. I can't bring myself to agree with them that if the bombs came here Papa would fix the house again. Nor can I say they will never come here. Instead I said, "That man (in the picture) couldn't build his house up again but he and the mama found a new place for the children."

Janna and Klaas seem to be handling the information well. (Klaas's bomb demonstration was very matter-of-fact, and we answered it as matter-of-factly, "Oh, yeh?" — and he went on to something else.) But I'm not feeling confident at all. Should I be more reassuring? Should I avoid certain subjects?[1]

The mother who raised this issue and asked these questions was pointing out more than a strategy concern, more than a "How-do-I-handle-this?" plea. She was also bringing up a central issue today for all parents, including parents of very young children: How do we enable our children to cope and flourish as peaceful people in a world permeated by violence?

A person would have to be comatose in today's world not to recognize the overwhelming presence of violence in every aspect of our lives. Newspapers and TV news are filled with stories of domestic abuse and other violent crimes, terrorism, violent repression, the loss of life because of a lack of basic services, and war itself. Some of these stories are directly connected to young children — who die in homes set afire by arsonists, who are victims of brutal treatment by abusive parents or caregivers, who are sometimes shot or killed by guns accidentally available in homes, who die in astonishingly rising rates from malnutrition and lack of basic health care, and who are the most innocent victims of wars.

Besides evidence of the rise in real violence in our world, our young children deal on a daily basis with a truly alarming rise in violence in TV shows and toys aimed specifically at them. According to the National Coalition on Television Violence, "the average American four-to-eight-year-old child this year will see some 250 episodes of war cartoons and 800 ads for war toys, all produced for toy companies to help sell war toys. This is the equivalent to 22 days of classroom instruction time in war thinking for the average American child."[2]

War cartoons average 41 acts of violence per hour with an attempted murder every two minutes. This kind of violent cartoon programming in the U.S. has increased from 1.5 hours a week in 1982 to 43 hours a week in 1987.[3] Since it is estimated that the average child watches three thousand hours of television by the age of five, most U.S. children are clearly touched very often by violence, even if it is in a "fantasy" form.

There are three principal problems with this real-but-not-real everyday violence for young children: increased aggressive behavior, desensitization about war, and conditioning for war.

Increases in Aggressive Behavior

Parents have told us repeatedly that they see an immediate reaction from their young children after they have watched a cartoon or another show with a high level of violence. A pre-school teacher from New Mexico looks at it this way:

> Many young children in day-care centers around the country are regularly acting out fantasies from today's most popular cartoons and television dramas. It is not an uncommon experience to suddenly hear a young four-year-old from the opposite end of the playground yell, "I'm going to get you, sucker," run full speed across the yard, leap onto an unsuspecting child, grab him or her by the neck, and throw them to the ground. When questioned about such aggressive behavior, the child looks up with that all-too-familiar innocent face and says, "But teacher, I'm Mr. T," or "I'm He-Man, Master of the Universe."[4]

Desensitization about the Human Consequence of War

One exchange I had with two of our children when they were six and eight still stays with me. The children and I were driving to a shopping center. On the way we passed the offices and plant of an aircraft manufacturer in our area, whose main business was in military contracts. The children asked what kind of work people did there.

In answering their questions, I included my opinion about the defense industry. I said I wished a company like this would use more of its resources making commercial airplanes and other peace-related items. I said I wished they did not make bombers and fighter planes.

The responses of Tommy and David were straightforward: "We have to have bombs! We have to be able to get the enemy so they can't get us. Bombs will help us fight!"

As we talked, I became aware of two underlying themes in what they were saying: (1) they saw the world with an "us-against-them" view; (2) they had little grasp of the totality of the destructiveness of war. They felt that somehow bombs would pick out the "bad people." It had not occurred to them that real bombs kill real children.

This experience occurred *before* the dramatic rise in the war toys and cartoons that are with us today. Today the situation is even more challenging because children see so much more violence, but with so little opportunity or capacity for understanding the real consequences. Somehow they need to be made aware that people do not get up again and walk away after they have been machine-gunned or bombed. While it is not advisable to show pre-school children pictures of the devastation of war, they do need some injection of realism from us, perhaps a comment like, "Looking at bombs makes me feel very sad because I think of people being killed."

Conditioning for War

Dr. Michael Rothenberg, a pediatrician and child psychiatrist at the University of Washington, has this overall assessment of war toys: "Parents need to realize the major objection to war toys is that they condition children to accept something unacceptable. If, as adults, they try to use these weapons to settle differences, they will fail, and the human race will be the victim."[5]

If children continually experience that the way people settle their very real differences, either interpersonally or internationally, is by throwing a knife or a throwing star, pulling out a pistol or a submachine gun, or dropping a bomb, they will be more likely to accept that method of solving conflicts as adults.

Another issue with regard to the oversaturation of children by images of violence is the kind of "enemy thinking" that these images at times initiate and always encourage. Several currently popular children's toys contain the word "enemy" on the packaging, labelling certain figures as "the enemy." My concern about this kind of labelling is that it begins a way of thinking in children. They are encouraged to think in terms of other people and other nations as their "enemy." Once you've made people your enemy, you don't have to worry about their welfare. You can destroy them or their area without guilt because that's "the enemy."

When everything else we do with young children is aimed at helping them develop friendship skills, it seems especially paradoxical to have toys that encourage them to think of others as their enemy. There is a need for children to develop personal safety skills, but this skill development does not mean regularly thinking that there are enemies for them to conquer.

Given the omnipresence of violence in our lives, the task of devising strategies to deal with this violence as we relate to our young children becomes an urgent challenge. Again, some of the strategies are more specific to our lives as adults and others to our interaction with children.

In this area, as in many others, to look at our own behavior and attitudes is not easy. The rewards are a heightened understanding of ourselves, a greater sensitivity to the effects of violence in our society, a more critical eye with regard to TV viewing, and an increased understanding of our own attitudes towards war and the preparation for war.

ADULT STRATEGIES

Violence in Our Language and Behavior

Young children are great imitators. In many respects, our words become their words, our deeds, their deeds. Therefore, it is helpful for us to look at our own words, expressions, and behavior with regard to violence. A few questions to ask ourselves:

- Do our children overhear us using violent expressions when talking to other adults, children, or even to them (for example, "punch your lights out," "kick his butt," "slap you silly," "hit you so hard you won't be able to sit down for a week")?

- What about our response to frustrating situations — drivers who cut us off, people who bump into us, long waits because of inefficiency? Do we overreact with violent terminology or gestures to these situations?

- What is our attitude about revenge, "getting even" for some insult or injury? Do our children hear us talk about "getting people who have gotten us"? (This is a particularly important concept because so many of the "good guys" on TV shows, videos, and films are people who have no qualms about retaliation.)

Adult Entertainment

At the same time that there's been such an alarming rise in violence in children's TV programming, there has been a corresponding violence escalation in prime-time TV and in movies for adults. The National Coalition on Television Violence monitors TV shows regularly, checking for violent acts per hour of programming. The result of their monitoring in the period from January to March 1986 showed at least twenty-five prime-time programs with ten violent acts per hour or more, with as many as sixty-five per hour. It is estimated that the average American watches over six hours of prime-time network violence per week. Added to that is another six hours of violence on other channels and on cable stations.[6] Of course, home videos provide another opportunity for violence to come into the home.

This is not to say that there are not some good TV shows or movies that do contain non-gratuitous violence. But the sheer amount of violence that we expose ourselves to in the name of entertainment must have some impact on our thinking and our behavior. Sporting events where violence occurs in the stands as well as on the field or the rink are another example of adult behavior that is influenced by violence in entertainment. If we are concerned about the amount of violence in children's entertainment, we also need to look at our own forms of recreation, how they affect us, and how the effect on us will transfer to our young children.

Attitudes Toward War and the Military Resolution of Conflict

Our own thinking about war naturally has an impact on our children. The exercise on p. 81, taken from an educational booklet prepared by Pax Christi,[7] gives us one way to look at our attitudes.

An exercise such as this is not meant to point a finger or assess guilt, but rather to generate some questioning about how we do feel, to gently force us to come face to face with our own attitudes and then to begin to look at the reasons for those attitudes.

In the same booklet, Pax Christi outlines four basic positions people take with regard to war (see p. 82). Thinking through these positions can help us not only to clarify our attitudes but also to assess what kind of thinking about war our children are picking up from us.

STRATEGIES WITH CHILDREN

Dan is nine years old. He has grown up in a home that puts a strong emphasis on peace and on the need for each of us to

Russian missiles are headed toward ten American cities. There is not enough time to stop them. About 150 million Americans will die, including the president. The president can launch a counter-attack killing at least 150 million Russians, or do nothing. If you were president, would you:

_____ order the attack _____ do nothing _____ other

I would approve of a presidential candidate who promised never to use nuclear weapons, even in the event of an attack on this country.

_____ agree _____ disagree _____ other

It would be better to destroy Russia or China rather than be forced to live under a communist and atheistic nation.

_____ agree _____ disagree _____ other

I believe nuclear weapons are sinful.

_____ agree _____ disagree _____ other

Sinful or not, nuclear weapons are a necessity.

_____ agree _____ disagree _____ other

Personally, I feel safer knowing that the United States is a nuclear power.

_____ agree _____ disagree _____ other

It wouldn't bother me if the United States fell behind the Soviet Union in nuclear weapon production and development.

_____ agree _____ disagree _____ other

ARE YOU SATISFIED WITH YOUR RESPONSES?

_____

_____

_____

take responsibility to bring about peace. It was the day of Dan's birthday party and one of his friends had given him a Transformer (a toy that can be changed from, e.g., an automobile into a ferocious robot). Somehow in the chaos and

shuffle of the party, the Transformer got lost. When Dan and
his mother finally got to the point of admitting that it was
lost, Dan's response was, "Oh well, it just got turned into a
plowshare."

We are not saying that the strategies we employ with our pre-
schoolers will guarantee us a nine-year-old who will be busy turn-
ing swords into plowshares, but there are rewarding moments and
those moments should be highlighted.

_____

_____ War is immoral; therefore, I cannot ever fight or support
a war.

_____ Some wars are just; others unjust. Therefore, I could
fight in and support some wars but not others. In some
cases I would even support the use of limited nuclear
weapons if they were used on military targets.

_____ Some wars are just; but not others. However, I draw the
line with nuclear weapons. I believe that it is wrong to
use and possess nuclear weapons.

_____ Some wars are just; others unjust. Therefore, I could
fight in and support some wars but not others. However,
I draw the line with nuclear weapons and believe it is
wrong to use them. I am not against the possession of
nuclear weapons at this time, because I think they stop
our enemies from using them.[8]

_____

The ideas that we offer fall into three broad categories: looking
at children's play patterns, dealing with the messengers of violence
that come into our home, and building a spirit of global interdependence.

Competition

Many educators, counselors, and psychologists, as well as other
social analysts, continue to question the pervasiveness of the competitive ethic in our culture. Few question competition totally,
for there is a good that comes from the effort expended to reach
a goal, from the physical and mental discipline that is a part of

many athletic endeavors. However, as I heard on the news report about the U.S. victory in the America Cup race, "One thing you can say for sure, Americans really like winning!"

It is the overemphasis on winning, on being the best, No. 1, on being better than someone else that we feel has relevance in a discussion about dealing with violence and a war mentality in children. While young children are not often engaged in organized competition as are older children, the basis for their attitudes begins early.

Nathan, at age six, was loving his role as goalie on his first-grade soccer team. The team had been practicing for their big debut for several weeks. The Saturday of the first game came, and Nathan headed off to play with unbridled enthusiasm. When he returned from the game, his attitude was still the same. His dad's first question, "How was the game?" was answered quickly, "Oh, it was great! We tied 2–2. *Nobody lost!*"

There are some general guidelines for us as parents regarding competitive or potentially competitive situations that can help us build on experiences like Nathan's.

- Emphasize the joy of playing or doing the activity, rather than the outcome. "Did you have fun kicking the ball?" "Did you like building the tower?" "Your car really runs fast!" "I bet it feels good to pedal your tricycle real fast like that!" "You're a great climber!" These comments are different from setting up a competitive way of thinking in young children by immediately asking them whether they did *better than* someone else — "Did you win the race?" "Did the teacher like your tower the best?" "Does your car go faster than hers?"

- Encourage situations where children almost naturally cooperate with each other, e.g., working together with blocks or trucks, building monuments in the sand, or preparing a family or group hero sandwich. The egocentric nature of young children makes cooperative endeavors only partially successful most of the time. But if children know that the adults value cooperation, that will have a bearing on their willingness to try to work and play with others.

- Point out to children ways in which people in the community do cooperate, e.g., construction workers, workers in a fast food restaurant, members of a team or choir.

- Avoid comparing one child's efforts to another's: "You can do a better job than that. Look how nicely Billy drew his picture." "Notice how quietly Ben is sitting. Why can't you do that?"

- Develop new games or rechannel old ones so that cooperation rather than competition is the key element. Jackie Haessly, in her book *Peacemaking,* offers the following criteria for evaluating both adults' and children's games in terms of cooperation:

  - When the games are played, are the participants laughing with, not at, each other?

  - Is the laughter contagious?

  - Does the activity allow for full participation by most persons? Or are several persons or large numbers standing around awaiting their turn?

  - Can the activity be modified to include persons with age, skill, physical, or mental limitations? If so, how?

  - Does the activity challenge all persons to work together for a common end?

  - Do good feelings or bad feelings dominate during or at the end of the activity?[9]

I had a personal experience with the last criterion in this list that has helped me to look more carefully at my attitude toward games in general. I was helping to organize a Halloween Party for the young children in our church family. After the Haunted House and apple-bobbing, we played Musical Chairs — which I thought was a perfectly innocent game for people of all ages. I shall never forget a three-year-old girl standing there after she had lost her seat, with tears streaming down her face. "This was supposed to be *fun!*" I thought. "What happened?" Of course, what happened was that Emily lost and was therefore excluded. I have since learned a cooperative way to play musical chairs:

"*Musical Laps*" (presented by Sandra Cangiano, at an Abington Friends School faculty workshop): The whole group forms a circle, all facing in one direction, close together, each with hands on the waist of the person ahead. When the music starts, everyone begins to walk forward. When the music stops, everyone sits down in the lap of the person to the rear. If the whole group succeeds in sitting in laps without anyone falling to the floor, the group wins. If people fall down, gravity wins. This works best with more than ten people about the same size (a big man will have a hard time sitting in the lap of a six-year-old!).[10]

Stephanie Judson details several other cooperative games specifically applicable to young children in her book *A Manual on Nonviolence and Children.* Several examples:

- *"Touch Nose"* (adapted from Touch Blue by Kathy Allen, day-care coordinator): This is an excellent activity for very young children. They must find a partner and sit or stand close together. Then the adult calls out different parts of the body (e.g., "touch nose") and the children touch each other's noses with their hands or fingers. The adult picks the different parts of the body to be touched.

- *"Kangaroo Hop"* (created by two teachers, Sandy Branam and Kathy Young): This is an energetic tag game used to let out excess energy, and it is also a lót of fun! If someone gets tagged, he or she is lucky. The lucky person becomes a kangaroo and hops around, trying to tag someone else. As soon as the next person is tagged, that person joins the first person in hopping around and tagging others. In the end, everyone is a lucky hopping kangaroo!

- *"Musical Hugs"* (adapted from Switchbacks by Gail Wooten): Small children seem to enjoy this tremendously. Children walk around the room while music is playing or the leader is singing. When the music stops, everyone hugs another person. The music starts up again and the whole process is repeated. The teacher can suggest that they hug a different person each time. As a variation try touching backs or elbows when the music stops.

- *"Corners"* (also adapted by Sandy Branam and Kathy Young): This game has been used successfully to start young children thinking about choices in solving problems. The choices might begin with, "Which would you rather be — ice cream or cake?" or "blocks or tricycles?" They then go to one side of the room or the other, according to their choice. Next, the leader could try more thoughtful issues like, "Would you rather be a biter or a slapper?" Since neither is very appealing, the children start to think. Having them talk with each other about the reasons for their choices involves them naturally in a discussion about the issues.[11]

Dealing with Television

Concerns about television among parents, educators, and psychologists are many. They range from an awareness of the kind of passivity that television induces, to the lack of encouragement of creativity and imagination, to the rapidity with which images change, to the impact of stereotypes based on race, sex, religion, age, and disability, to the effects of violence on a young child's thinking and behavior.

While there is no one strategy that works for every family in dealing with television, several suggestions follow.

Monitor the TV shows aimed primarily at very young children. The National Coalition on Television Violence[12] sends regular mailings to keep their readers updated on current developments in violence and the media — mostly TV, but other media as well. As of February 1987, their monitoring concluded that the most violent cartoon shows were as follows:

Name of Show	Violent Acts/Hour
Photon	114
Inhumanoids	86
Centurions/Power Extreme	85
G.I. Joe	84
Challenge of the Gobots	66

Among the *least violent* cartoon shows were:

Kids, Incorporated	Berenstain's Bears
Punky Brewster	Get Along Gang
Alvin and the Chipmunks	

The result of any kind of monitoring should be some firm guidelines for children about what they can or cannot watch. One couple we know with children ranging from pre-schoolers to teens kept their TV in the closet, so the decision to watch it was very intentional with a lot of effort required. They said it cut down considerably on the practice of just switching on the set because there wasn't anything else to do. In our own family we have tried to operate on a flexible schedule of a maximum of seven hours a week for TV watching. I say "have tried" because the scheduling has gotten more complicated as the children have gotten older. When they were younger it was easier to state the limit and encourage them to choose their hour each day.

Mr. Rogers, the well-known TV educator and beloved friend of many pre-schoolers, has this suggestion for the times when our children do see something violent on TV:

Children can learn to cope with many scary things in life — violence on television included — so long as they have caring adults at hand who want to help them. Watching television with our children, and talking about it, is the best way to keep violence on television from becoming overwhelming and damaging. We may even be able to turn whatever violence our children do see into a positive experience, so long as we see it with them. We can, for instance, use it to help our children identify feelings, strengthen their own sense of self-control, sort out what's real and what's pretend, understand family values, understand more about cause and effect, and learn more about how the real world works.

Asking a child how he or she feels about a scary, violent TV episode can be the beginning of really important talk. Televised violence can arouse deep and strong feelings in all of us, but it takes young children a long time to identify such feelings as grief, anger, or fright in themselves, and even longer to learn to manage these feelings. Children need adult help. If you let your child know how you have similar feelings, and can talk about them, you can help your child learn to identify them too. You might want to talk about the violent adult behavior that you see on television, about how scary it can be when you feel so angry that you want to hurt someone, about a recent time when you helped your child

stop before doing something hurtful, or about a time when
you were proud of your child for finding a constructive way
of expressing angry feelings. This kind of talk supports his
or her own growing capacities for self-control.[13]

Mr. Rogers's suggestions provide a basis for critical viewing
habits. I would take them a step further and actually tell a child
what I did or didn't like about an entire show or about some particular incident on the show, e.g., "I think too many people get
hurt on this show." "I wish they would talk to each other instead
of hitting." "Why do all those people have guns?" "It scares me
when I see people pretend to kill other people on television."

Taking our concerns one more step, we can tell our children
that we're going to write a letter to the station or the sponsor and
express our opinion, and perhaps invite them to sign the letter.

Toys

The selection of and encouragement toward certain kinds of toys
can be one of the most rewarding and exciting yet challenging
aspects of parenthood. None of us is ever completely successful in
convincing our children to play with the kinds of toys that we value,
but our consistent interest in our children's toys is very important
for them because toys are such a major part of their world.

When our children were very young I wondered about our insistence on not buying guns for them. Two incidents stand out in
my mind. One involved a visit to a friend's home during which
Tom became almost hysterical because one of the other little boys
was pointing a gun at David, saying he was going to shoot him.
After lots of reassurance from us that this was not a real gun and
that Andy was not going to harm David, Tom was able to calm
down and resume his play.

But the incident resurfaced about six months later. Tom had
just turned six and had had another experience of feeling intim-
idated by the gun-play of other children. He said to Jim, "Dad,
I have to have a gun. I have to defend myself." Jim attempted
to suggest a solution that would meet his needs of self-defense
but would not involve getting a gun. He said, "What if I make a
bullet-proof shield for you? Then you'll be protected." Tom stated
emphatically, "That won't work, I have to have a gun!" Then he
had a thought, and offered his own compromise, "How about a

squirt gun? That just shoots water. It doesn't even shoot pretend bullets."

We were struck by his ability to honor our values, yet come up with a way to meet his own needs. He got his squirt gun, and soon afterwards gun-playing ceased to be an issue in the neighborhood. But the questions about gun-play and about toys and violence in general did not cease to be an issue for us, as well as for many other parents.

Aaron is four years old. When his mother confronted him with her displeasure about his fascination over war toys, his answer was simple and, in his own mind, very clear-cut, "Mommy, I don't like war. I just like the toys." In this same family the parents, Nanette and Jim, have been clear about their not wanting weapons in their home. They relented somewhat at one point and allowed Aaron to have a Transformer, but they said the robot's weapon would have to go. They made a little ceremony of disposing of the weapon, with what Nanette says was mixed success. Aaron had accepted the family's rule, but he still grieved over the loss of the weapon.

In Aaron's mind the difference between war itself and his toys may be very real, but that's not necessarily the case for all children. How to deal with the growing popularity of war toys and other weapon toys is a perplexing question for all of us.

The General Board of Church and Society of the United Methodist Church has published a booklet called, "Parents' Guide to Non-Violent Toy-Buying." They recommend guidelines for selection relevant to all toys, but also help us ask ourselves questions as we decide whether to purchase a particular war toy:

- Look the toys over carefully and think about their purpose. What will the child be learning from the use of this toy?
- Read the packaging! What is the attitude toward life promoted by this toy?
- What is the toy's play value? Can it be used again and again in a variety of ways? Is it appropriate for this child's age level? Will it isolate the child or assist him or her in social development?
- Does it help the child to develop imagination without him or her being lost in a world of overwhelming fantasy?
- Does it assist the child in learning to cope with and bring order to the real world?

- Would I feel comfortable being involved in the child's play with this toy?
- Are the concepts presented by the toy appropriate for the child?
- What are the values promoted by the toy? Does it promote concern for humankind? Does it allow for the development of positive values? Is it in tune with what I want my child to grow up to be?[14]

Other strategies with regard to toys and play involving toys are as follows:

Critiquing the Toys

It's essential that we clarify for ourselves our own feelings and thinking about weapons as toys, as well as the reasons for those feelings. We used to tell our children that we didn't think it was fun to pretend to kill people and that it made us uncomfortable, maybe even scared, when we saw children pointing guns at each other. This was prior to the days when there were "laser artillery weapons," "motorized water submachine guns," "assault copters" and "S.A.V.A.G.E. strike cycles" on the shelves. We were dealing mostly with guns, rifles, and a few other military toys. The question above — "Would I feel comfortable being involved in the child's play with this toy?" — is very telling. How would I feel about pointing a gun at or dropping a bomb on my child?

One parent used the analogy of drug paraphernalia when thinking about weapons. She said, "Would we buy our children a syringe and a needle or give them a little baggie filled with powdered sugar so they could pretend to deal in drugs? Obviously not! We would be appalled by the idea! Why then do we encourage them to pretend to kill people in other ways?"

Probably the most important issue involved in whether to purchase war toys for our child is that *every time we purchase a toy we communicate an adult value to the child who receives that toy.* Four-year-old Peter has parents who have very strong beliefs about not buying guns or other war toys for him, and they have been consistent in their refusal without making guns a forbidden fruit in their homes. Peter, however, makes guns out of other things and has said very clearly to his parents, "You don't like guns, but I do." Peter's situation is a good example of the world of difference between making guns out of sticks, Lego blocks, bread crusts, or fingers, and being handed a gun by an adult who is a significant person in a child's life. Mr. Rogers puts it this way:

What is important is not so much whether our children engage in gun play, but whether they know how we feel about it — or about anything else they do. Our children need us to be able to make rules that express our values and help ensure their safety.... It is from the people they love the most that children acquire so many of their values.[15]

So Peter has the advantage of knowing what his parents' values are. At this point he's choosing to operate from a different perspective, but he is very clear about his parents' position.

Another way to develop a critical attitude toward toys is simply to ask probing questions of our children in order to find out why they like a certain toy. Is it, for example, because a friend has it, or because it makes them feel strong, or because they like the action and the excitement?

Dealing with Peers

"But all the other kids have Inhumanoids!" (or G.I. Joe, or Rambo, or ...). "My mother-in-law was buying guns for my son from the day he was born." How often we hear these comments from ourselves or others. The question is how to help our children deal with substantial pressure either from other children or from other significant adults in their lives.

Some families have a specific and well-publicized policy in their home. It is a "War-Toys-Free-Zone" policy that means that no war toys are allowed. So other children must check their guns, killer robots, and bomber planes at the door.

Curtis and Denise are a couple who have a "no-war-toys" policy in their home. When their twins, Jeffrey and Sharon, had a birthday party, the parents were worried that some of the guests would bring war toys as gifts. So they printed on the invitations the words "NO WAR TOYS, PLEASE." To their relief, all the other children complied. Those kinds of initiatives are not always met with acceptance by others, but sometimes the results surprise us and our children.

Alternatives

As with other aspects of peacemaking, the emphasis in any discussion of children's toys should be on what we're *for* rather than
merely on what we're against. In other words, if we are telling our
children and others family members that we're not comfortable
with toy weapons, what are we suggesting as alternatives?

A key to choosing a *realistic* alternative to a war toy is that the
toy must fulfill some of the same needs that the action-oriented war
toys do. Dolores Kirk is an experienced early childhood educator
who has done work in this area. She has concluded from her own
research, as well as her firsthand experience, that there are three
characteristics of children's play that need to be acknowledged and
nurtured in any attempt to provide alternatives to weapons toys:
motion, strength, and speed. She suggests cars that can move
at a fast rate, with ramps to accelerate that speed, and any opportunity to exercise strength — lifting boxes, moving chairs, etc.
She also suggests play patterns that involve the child in an exercise of *power,* e.g., when the children in her class play police,
they do so with tablets in hand so they can write out a traffic
summons. They also block off pretend streets and highways with
traffic zones — which provides an enormous sense of power, yet one
that doesn't involve weapons. Playing in sand and making dams
that will reroute the course of water poured into the sand area is
another way for children to exercise power or control over their
play environment.

That need for control over the environment is central to all
weapons play. Mr. Rogers reflects on this:

> Guns seem to confer a kind of superpower because they can
> make things happen at a distance, as though your arms were
> enormously long. Perhaps for this same reason, remote-
> control toys like train sets or battery-driven cars often have a
> powerful attraction for young children. Certainly water pis-
> tols confer real power, and many of us can remember how
> hard it was not to squirt someone with the garden hose when
> we were meant to be watering the flowers or washing the
> car. Even flashlights have this power, and are reassuring to
> children who are afraid of the dark.[16]

His comments point to several alternatives: flashlights, remote con-
trolled vehicles, trains, water hoses, etc.

Tools are yet another important alternative. They give the child a very real sense of power — the ability to create a new entity. Also, of course, they call for strength and motion. Many parents find that it is not necessary to buy child-size tools. Adult tools, with supervision and with the right sized nails and soft wood, can provide good opportunities for success.

Other alternative toys, gleaned from lists compiled by *Alternatives,* the United Methodist Church, and the Peace Resource Center of San Diego, include:

- Lego Blocks
- Child Guidance Toys
- Play Skool — including Lincoln Logs and Bristle Blocks
- Fisher-Price Adventure People and other toys. (Caution: one of the Fisher-Price Construx Sets is a military toy)
- Tonka trucks
- Planetariums and aquariums
- Musical instruments
- Stuffed animals
- Dolls and puppets
- Balls and other sports equipment
- Office-type toys
- Slinkies and puzzles
- Bikes and trikes
- Clay, paints, crayons, scissors, and paper
- Wooden blocks[17]

While all these are not in the category of motion, strength, speed, or power toys, they do provide stimulation of the senses and opportunities for creativity and imagination. In one sense, there is really no end to these types of toys. The important element is to focus on what we want the toy to encourage or foster in the child — creativity, imagination, a sense of nurturing, problem-solving, coordination, development of both fine and gross motor skills, strength, and, probably most important, *Fun!*

Expressing Our Opinions to Toy Makers, Buyers, and Stores

The following is an excerpt from a letter written to Coleco Industries about their line of Rambo toys:

> It has come to my attention that Coleco Industries plans to market a Rambo doll. I read a short news article...which quoted your spokesperson, Barbara Wruck, as saying the doll will come with "weaponry and vehicles, all the things that create a proper play environment."
>
> I am a mother of two children, and I am also a Vietnam veteran. I served fifteen months in 1968 and 1969 at an evacuation hospital near Saigon. I believe this qualifies me to address this issue with you.
>
> Mr. Clarke, I seriously doubt the wisdom of your plans to market this line.... The Rambo movie is R-rated, so not to be seen by children....
>
> The movie was so full of violence as to be pornographic, but it was awfully tame compared to the real thing. No scenes showed exit wounds, for instance. With high-velocity weapons there are exit wounds much, much worse than those of entry. A gun-shot wound to the forehead results in the back of the head being blown away. Also, few injured died immediately, or so quietly, or to the tune of martial music. They scream and moan and clutch and squirm grotesquely. Their belly wounds are blown full of whatever muck and trash is near them, and they suffer miserably. Now, do you want to hear about burns? People do not die immediately of their burns either. Needless to say, I have only touched the surface. So how are you going to depict all this within the context of a "proper play environment"?[18]

Most of us do not have this writer's experience, but we can write to express our opinion and include our children by asking them what they feel we should say. Even pre-schoolers enjoy having their opinions solicited.

Many communities have sponsored boycotts of war toys with leafletting of shopping areas. While I feel it is important to exercise caution in involving young children in any kind of public action, if you as the parent feel they understand enough of what you're leafletting about and if they want to join you, then it can be a good experience for the family. I must admit, however, that when our children were young, we found that their initial enthusiasm waned very quickly. "I'm tired" or "I'm hungry" or "I want to go home" came all too soon.

Learning about the Global Family

A couple from New Mexico reflected on their young daughter's perceptions about war in this way:

The first time my daughter (age three) asked about war was during the El Salvador situation before the March 1982 elections. She saw on the news all the soldiers and fighting and asked what was happening. I explained as simply as I could. Her one and only response was, "God must be very sad." The second incident happened at an anti-nuclear rally in a park. One display showed dolls that had been burnt as depicting the aftermath of nuclear war. Meghan seemed really stunned by it yet wanted to keep looking. Again, I tried to explain as simply as I could what bombs were and what they could do. She just looked at me and said, "Mommy, govnants [governments] should use words." I guess my feelings from these exchanges are that as we incorporate the principles of non-violent conflict resolution in our homes (as best we can, being fallen creatures), our children can be trusted to form some simple yet profound conclusions on their own — even three-year-olds.[19]

A mentality that accepts war as inevitable is fostered by "us-against-them" thinking. Counter to that is a global interdependence mentality — we are all part of one global family, different in some ways, alike in others, and all striving to care about each other and to learn to live together in harmony. There are several ways to translate that for young children.

Language

Learning to respect languages other than English is an important aspect of global understanding, even for the very young. Certainly if there is another language spoken in the home, young children need to be exposed to that language. Our daughter, Theresa, as a pre-schooler, used to comment about other people who speak English with an accent. Her initial reaction was often, "Why does she talk so funny?" When we explained to her that that person could speak two languages and had talked for a longer period of time in the other language, she seemed to begin to see that bilingual ability in a positive light.

The TV show *Sesame Street* does a good job of helping children deal with Spanish-English language differences. They are presented to children as a normal part of living with other people. ("I say it this way. You say it this other way.") For young children, learning simple words and phrases for "good morning," "good-bye," "my name is," and the like in several languages can help to minimize fears and to develop feelings of respect for other languages and hence other people. As pre-schoolers our children enjoyed two books by Muriel Feelings, *Jambo Means Hello* and *Moja Means One.* The books are Swahili alphabet and counting books, wonderfully illustrated. Folkway Records has a series by Ella Jenkins that effectively introduces young children to language differences.

Learning about Other People

Since pre-schoolers thrive on experiential learning, there are a myriad of possible ways to expose them to other peoples around the world right within our home.

- Having a world map up somewhere in the home enables us to point to the different areas of the world as we're talking about them, and of course to give the children some sense of distance. Another option is a globe. An inflatable globe ball is an especially attractive one for pre-schoolers because it can also be a toy — tossed around while you sing, "We've got the whole world in our hands."[20]

- Place mats, calendars, flags, or pictures on the wall can internationalize the atmosphere of our homes. Church World Services, Catholic Relief Services, and the Holy Childhood Association all have beautiful global family calendars. Your local United Nations Association and the UNICEF office in New York are sources for many different kinds of visual aids, flags, pictures, and greeting cards. Many communities also have Third World handicraft outlets that provide similar items with the assurance that the money for the purchases goes to the craftspeople in the Third World nations.[21]

• Experimenting with foods from different countries can provide an enjoyable celebrative time for "pretending we're in Italy, Ghana, China...." We try to do that once a month in our own family, and we combine the meal with music (records from the public library) and a look at pictures from library books. Children love a party atmosphere!

• When Theresa was in pre-school her class celebrated UN Day (October 24) by talking about the purpose of the United Nations Organization and by reciting the World Pledge:

> I pledge allegiance to the World
> To cherish every living thing,
> To care for earth and sea and air,
> With peace and freedom everywhere![22]

Families can also celebrate UN Day, a time for us to think of ourselves more consciously as members of a global family. The celebration of that day could be an opportunity for talking with the children about "peace" as the purpose of the United Nations. A postcard or picture of the UN building or the UN flag is an effective visual aid for the celebration.

• We feel it is particularly important, as part of our learning about other peoples of the world, to spend time "visiting" the Soviet Union. The Fellowship of Reconciliation (Box 271, Nyack, NY 10960) has a beautiful set of photos of Soviet children, available as posters, post cards, and a calendar. They also have a number of suggested projects, all aimed at undercutting the concept of the Soviet people as our enemies.

Children's Fears about War

More and more has been written in the past several years about the growing concern among young people about the possibility of nuclear war. Some of the concern is evident even in pre-schoolers. Robert J. Lifton, M.D., Professor of Psychiatry at Yale University Medical School, has been one of the foremost researchers in this area. With regard to pre-schoolers he has said, "This imagery of nuclear extinction begins in young people at the age of four or five years — it doesn't wait for adulthood — they can't help but take in this imagery." [23]

Following are guidelines for effective ways to handle the fears of young children about war:

- Be aware that children's egocentrism can quite naturally provide them a natural defense against despair. For example, a child may think, "If I tell the president we want peace, we'll have peace." It's appropriate to build on that without giving children a false sense of power; rather, let them know that their ideas, posters, or letters are important.

- Children always need assurance that they will be protected by adults. Nancy Carlsson-Paige and Diane Levin make this point strongly in their book *Helping Young Children Understand Peace, War and the Nuclear Threat*. In remarks directed primarily to the classroom teacher, they say that in response to a child's question like "Is a bomb going to drop on us?" a teacher could say,

  "A bomb is not going to drop on us now. You are safe here." A hug and then some special help getting involved in a classroom activity could provide tangible reassurance to the child that she is safe and cared for. Such reassurance, which reaffirms the child's safety in the immediate moment and confirms the adult's ability to provide a secure environment for the child, is almost always the most helpful kind of reassurance. [24]

  The same idea, of course, applies to parents.

- Because young children are more attuned to the concrete than the abstract, war is usually easier for them to picture than peace. One of our tasks is to make peace more concrete. Encourage children to respond freely to the following:

  - What color would you color peace? Love? Happiness?
  - What do you suppose love tastes like? Peace?
  - I wonder how peace would feel if you would touch it — hold it?
  - Show me with your body: What does joy or happiness mean to you? Let your body to the talking. How about love? Peace?

  – Suppose everyone on the globe was happy, living in love
  and peace. How do you think the sky would look? Feel?
  What sounds would you hear? What smells would you
  smell?

• We can also make peace more concrete by using "peace language" with children. "You certainly were a peacemaker in
  the park today," "Anne, when you made room for Tammy at
  the sand table, you were being a peacemaker." "That was
  a very peaceful way to solve that problem." Such comments
  can help children begin to sense that peace and peacemaking
  are active pursuits.

Admittedly this issue of children and the violence in the world
around them is a complex one. As we write, there are new toys
being produced that, through the technology of computer chips,
will allow children to interact with military combat scenarios on
TV programs and actually participate in the killing. And violence
in the real world continues to destroy and injure some children and
create an unstable world for all children. Whatever we do, we need
to nurture our own hope as well as our children's, and perhaps that
hope is best nurtured by listening to the voice of a child:

PEACE

Peace is caring for those around you.
Peace is all Nations joining hands
Peace is not destroying gods creation
Peace is knowing the meaning of love
Peace will only happen if everyone works together.
                                        —Sirena, age 10[25]

Notes

1. Excerpted from *Parenting for Peace and Justice Newsletter*, no. 5, Fall 1982,
p. 2.
   2. Press Release, National Coalition on Television Violence (NCTV), October 31, 1986.
   3. Ibid., November 26, 1985, and phone conversation with NCTV office,
February 1987.
   4. Craig Simpson, "The Violence of War Toys: He-Man, Voltron, Trans-
formers, and Gobots," *Nonviolent Activist*, November–December 1985, p. 3.
   5. "Values Through Toys," in *Newsletter for Peace and Justice Education Center*, 713 Monroe Ave., Rochester, NY 14607, p. 16.

6. *NCTV News,* vol. 7, nos. 5 and 6, June–July 1986, p. 6.

7. Mary Lou Kownacki, OSB, ed., *A Race to Nowhere: An Arms Race Primer for Catholics,* Pax Christi-USA, 348 East Tenth Street, Erie, PA 16503, 1982, p. 4.

8. Ibid., p. 64.

9. Jacqueline Haessly, *Peacemaking: Family Activities for Justice and Peace* (New York: Paulist Press, 1980), pp. 36–37.

10. Stephanie Judson, *A Manual on Nonviolence and Children,* Nonviolence and Children Program, Friends Peace Committee, 1515 Cherry St., Philadelphia, PA 19102, 1977, p. G–16.

11. Ibid., p. G–27.

12. National Coalition on Television Violence, P.O. Box 2157, Champaign, IL 61820 (usual membership donation, $25).

13. Fred Rogers and Barry Head, *Mister Rogers Talks with Parents* (New York: Berkley Books, 1983), p. 179.

14. "Parents Guide to Non-Violent Toy-Buying," The General Board of Church and Society, The United Methodist Church, 100 Maryland Ave., N.E., Washington, DC 20002, p. 8.

15. *Mister Rogers,* p. 120.

16. Ibid., p. 119.

17. Compiled from Alternatives, P.O. Box 429, Ellenwood, GA 30049; "Parents Guide to Non-Violent Toy-Buying" (cited above); and Peace Resource Center of San Diego, 5717 Lindo Paseo, San Diego, CA 92115 (caution note for Fisher-Price added by authors).

18. Personal correspondence of Mary Garrison, October 17, 1985, used with her permission.

19. *Parenting for Peace and Justice Newsletter,* no. 6, Winter 1982, p. 2.

20. Globes are available from several sources, including the office of the Parenting for Peace and Justice Network, 4144 Lindell, #122, St. Louis, MO 63108.

21. Originally from Women's International League for Peace and Freedom, 1213 Race St., Philadelphia, PA 19103.

22. Blanche Friedman, "Preschoolers' Awareness of Nuclear Threat," *Newsletter,* California Association for the Education of Young Children, vol. 12, no. 2, Winter 1984, p. 4.

23. Nancy Carlsson-Paige and Diane E. Levin, *Helping Young Children Understand Peace, War and the Nuclear Threat* (Washington, D.C.: National Association for the Education of Young Children, 1985), p. 19.

24. Gerald G. Jampolsky, ed., *Children as Teachers of Peace* (Millbrae, Calif.: Celestial Arts, 1982), p. 15.

Chapter 6

Rooted in Faith

"Children are teaching us what a source of joy it can be to have a God in our life."[1] With these words, Sofia Cavalletti, an authority on children's spirituality, points out a key element in a child's faith life — a deep, spirit-filled sense of joy. Throughout this book we have tried to recognize the necessity for that joyful spirit in a child's life, even as we looked at realities that prevent that joy from thriving — violence, racism, sexism, handicapism, ageism, and war. For the authors of this book, all the suggestions that we make on any specific issue have a basis in our experience of faith and in our understanding of a young child's joyful relationship with God. We realize that the readers of this book will come from many different faith bases. For this reason we chose to put our reflections about nurturing the spiritual development of children in relation to peace and justice issues into one chapter. For us, these reflections form an underpinning for what has been developed in the other chapters. We are hopeful that the strategies and ideas presented in this chapter will be seen as integrally connected to the previous chapters. In offering these ideas, we will be combining both adult strategies and strategies with children, but our primary focus will be on strategies with children.

There are three focal points for our suggestions about nurturing the faith of young peacemakers and agents for justice: a sense of wonder, a spirit of joy and celebration, and an experience of a deep trust and love.

WONDER

When was the last time you were really silly? When I asked
this question of participants in a workshop, one young mother
replied, "Ten years ago."

Thinking she had experienced then some terrible event
that traumatized her, I exclaimed, "Ten years ago! What
happened?"

"I had my first child," she replied. As I and others looked
at her blankly, she went on to explain, "I don't think parents
should be silly. If they are, they will lose control."

How sad, I thought. Yet, in my work on stress and the
family, I discovered this mother is not alone in her thinking.[2]

Dolores Curran, the noted family researcher, columnist, and
lecturer tells this story in a magazine article entitled "Rediscovering the Child Within." Even though being silly is not to be
equated with a sense of wonder, there is a similarity, especially
from a child's perspective. Probably our adult insistence on maintaining control (or thinking that we're maintaining control) is one
of our biggest impediments to developing our own and our child's
sense of wonder.

Carol Dittberner, a Montessori educator and catechist, provides
insight into manifestations of this sense of wonder:

> What do we know about the young child's religious life?
> What we have observed is pure joy. The most overwhelm-
> ing aspect of the young child's life is the *sense of wonder*.
> Children are filled with wonder at the tiniest bug, the softest
> rabbit, or a ride on a parent's knee. Their wonder is some-
> times filled with exclamation, but it is often silent. Children
> are led into contemplation of what is before them.
>
> Wonder is present in the adult's life also; it is what causes
> us to move in regard to something. Wonder urges us forward
> because it is the base of all creation, of the great reality and
> the great question, "Who has prepared all this for me?"[3]

If this is true, if wonder fills the life of a child and is also present
in our life, then we need only cultivate carefully what is already
there. The question Carol Dittberner poses, "Who has prepared
all this for me?" gives us an indication of some directions for our
"cultivation."

As we are encouraging children to respect the earth itself, we can do that in the context of our relationship to the Creator. "Look what God has given us!" It is our responsibility and our joy to take care of this earth because it belongs to the Lord. In Leviticus 25:23, God speaks very directly: "The land belongs to me, and to me you are only strangers and guests." So as we take walks in the park, examine rocks, and sit in awe of butterflies, we are constantly more aware of the "fullness of the Lord" and of the many ways that God has gifted us.

When Theresa was about two years old, we spent time talking to a Winnebago mother about what she did with her own children to reinforce in them their Winnebago heritage. We were looking for suggestions that we could follow in our own family. She said that the outdoors was extremely important to Winnebago people, but that it was not always necessary to be "doing something" outside. Rather she said she encouraged her children to just *be* when they were outside, to recognize and feel their oneness with nature and with God.

We have tried over the years to designate special places in the park for each one of the children, places where we could be quiet, enjoy the beauty of creation, open our hearts to God, and really allow our sense of wonder to expand.

As we marvel with children over buds on trees about to open, over a seedling pushing through the ground, over a new puppy, and certainly over a tiny baby, we are helping their sense of wonder to grow. We are, therefore, cultivating their relationship with God.

With young children we would not use the word "steward" or "stewardship," but we can certainly encourage that value with them. The earth and the resources of the earth are ours to use for the good of all. We need to take good care of what we have. So as we encourage young children to exercise care about their pets, their toys, and other people, we are encouraging them to be good stewards of God's earth. We are also providing them with the basis for a love of peace and a desire for the world to be free of war. A solid sense of respect for the earth and the earth's resources means that a child's concerns and questions about peace and war will come from a reverence for life rather than a fear of death.

Capitalizing on children's sense of wonder also gives us an opportunity to introduce them to the true spirit of wonder that is part of the Native American ethic. Pictures and picture books

of Native American people can reinforce this, as can using Chief
Seattle's prayer, which emphasizes respect for the earth and the
direct connection between care for the earth and responsibility to
the Creator.

Teach your children what we have taught our children, that
the earth is our mother. Whatever befalls the earth, befalls
the children of the earth. If we spit upon the ground, we spit
upon ourselves. This we know. The earth does not belong to
us; we belong to the earth. . . .
    One thing we know, which the white man may one day
discover — our God is the same God. You may think now
that you own God as you wish to own our land; but you
cannot. God is the God of *all* people, and God's compassion
is equal for all. This earth is precious to God, and to harm
the earth is to heap contempt on its Creator. . . .
    So love it as we have loved it. Care for it as we have cared
for it. And with all your strength, with all your mind, with
all your heart, preserve it for your children, and love . . . as
God loves us all.[4]

Anything that we do to encourage in young children a respect
for the variety in the human family is another way of building on
that sense of wonder. A collage of pictures of people with different
skin colors, different hair styles, different dress — all presented as
children of God — can be a visual reminder to a young child of the
beauty and richness in the differences that exist in God's family.
"Christ is like a single body, which has many parts; it is still one
body, even though it is made up of different parts" (1 Corinthians
12:12).

JOY AND CELEBRATION

What are peacemakers if they are not joyful, celebrative people?
In the same vein, Brother Gabriel Moran, F.S.C., describes Christianity, in a way that could apply also to other faith traditions:
"If Christian faith has a future it will issue from a way of looking
at the world that stimulates response, creativity, and passionate
involvement."[5]

    At the core of a pre-schooler's being is "response, creativity,
and passionate involvement." As we seek to make peace and justice

values more at the core of our lives as well as our children's, we need to connect peace and justice with a spirit of joyful living. Have "peace parties" to celebrate the birthdays of peace heroes like St. Francis of Assisi, Dorothy Day, and Martin Luther King, Jr. One mother suggested special treats for peaceful resolution of conflict in the backyard or on the playground. Peace songs and dances always add to a celebrative atmosphere. Music and art and movement and puppetry need to be seen much more as connected to working for peace and justice. The following is one simple puppet skit, "Peace Soup," taken from *Puppets for Peace* by Camy Condon and James McGinnis:

- Using any kind of hand puppet, although a cook with a large soup spoon is most appropriate, announce to the children that you are making "peace soup." They ask, "pea soup?" "No," you say, "*peace* soup!" If they ask again, "pea soup?" you answer, "No, *peace* soup!"

- Ask them for some of the ingredients for "peace soup" and with each answer say "one cupful of..." whatever ingredient is voiced — love, listening, forgiveness, sharing, praying, marching, etc. If you think one or more are especially appropriate, you could say "*two* cupsful of" that ingredient.

- After filling the hypothetical pot with these ingredients, have your hand puppet stir the peace soup and declare: "peace is delicious!"[6]

Special religious celebration times are also opportunities for rejoicing together as the people of God, as well as opportunities for learning more about another culture or faith tradition. Lillian is a Jewish grandmother who reflects this way on the celebration of Chanukah:

One of the holidays readily accessible to the young is Chanukah, or Festival of Lights. It commemorates a great moment in our history, but more than that. It is a time to re-dedicate ourselves to human betterment. Thus the children from infancy on observe the candle-lighting ceremony and are encouraged and, later, required to make one or more wishes, statements, or observations, differing each year, as they light the candles for the eight nights. Or, the family together makes up the eight "directions" for that year's agenda. They

can relate to self-betterment, interpersonal relationships, the
world's concerns. The feeling is that our Menorahs can help
eliminate pettiness, jealousy, insensitivity to others with gentle words, kind gestures, charitable deeds, support of those
in distress. The emphasis is that isolating oneself from the
world at large is contrary to our beliefs. The emphasis is
always on what would implement Peace and Justice![7]

Both Jewish and non-Jewish families can help their children grow
in an understanding of Jewish history and in a sense of responsibility for the broader world through the celebration of the festival
of Chanukah.

The celebration of Kwanza is another opportunity to reinforce
values, to enrich our family's prayer life, and to grow in an understanding of African and Afro-American traditions.

Kwanza begins on December 26th and ends on January 1st. It
is a special time for African-Americans to celebrate their families,
their African heritage, and their commitment to each other and to
the seven principles of Kwanza. Those principles are expressed by
African-American people in the following way:

- *Umoja,* Unity, to maintain unity in the family, community,
  and among all African peoples.

- *Kujichagulia,* Self-Determination, to define names ourselves,
  and to direct our own lives.

- *Ujima,* Collective Work and Responsibility, to work together
  and really care about each other.

- *Ujamaa,* Cooperative Economics, to share whatever we have,
  including the profits from our businesses, with each other.

- *Nia,* Purpose, to keep our minds on our purpose — the building and developing of our community so we may be truly free
  and independent people.

- *Kuuma,* Creativity, to nurture the creativity in all our people
  in order to constantly improve our communities.

- *Imani,* Faith, to maintain a belief in our collective strength
  and in the wisdom of our elders.

How can we participate in the celebration of Kwanza?

- Use the colors of Kwanza in decoration and explain their
  meaning:

- Black: for African and African-American people
- Red: for the struggle of African-American people
- Green: for land and hope

- Use this as a time to introduce or reintroduce your children to Black Americans whose lives have embodied the spirit of Kwanza, e.g., Rosa Parks, Fannie Lou Hamer, Martin Luther King, Jr., Paul Robeson, Ida B. Wells-Barnett (a good source for her story for older readers is *Black Foremothers: Three Lives,* Old Westbury, N.Y.: The Feminist Press, 1979).

- *The Story of Kwanza,* by Safisha L. Madhubuti, illustrated by Murry N. DePillars, Third World Press, 7424 S. Cottage Grove Ave., Chicago, IL 60619, 1977, is a good explanation of Kwanza for young readers.

- Take one principle for each day of Kwanza and decide on one concrete action as a family to live out that principle (e.g., Imani: set aside time for special family prayer, remembering elders in the family, living and dead).

- For a fuller explanation of the origin and the specifics of the celebration rituals for Black American families, consult "How I Came to Celebrate Kwanza," by Omonike Weusi-Puryeai in *Essence,* December 1979, pp. 112ff.

Some of the more traditional celebration times throughout the Christian church year are wonderful joy-filled times for young children. One example is Advent. To begin with, the lighting of the Advent candles is an important symbol for young children. Our family Advent tradition revolves around the manger as a symbol of simplicity and service. Several evenings each week we gather at the manger, which we have built. The children take turns lighting the candles, one for each week of Advent. We reflect on the day that has passed and on some way in which we each have been able to serve others that day. As each of us shares this service experience, we place a piece of straw in our crib to make a softer place for Jesus to lie. This is how we prepare for his coming. Prayer and a song conclude the short ceremony. The symbol and ritual have become an important part of our family's growing tradition.

Pat and Ed and their nine children also celebrate Advent in a service-oriented way. They pair with another family, and each regularly surprises the other with special prayers, notes, a visit,

simple homemade gifts, and a morning together chopping down
their Christmas trees. It makes Advent a time of joyful sharing for
both families.

Easter is a feast and a whole season when joy and celebration
are paramount in Christian religious experience. Dorothy Dixon
relates Easter to the young child in this way:

> When it is Easter season, it is time to celebrate "God's prom-
> ise of new life." All the world is a parable of this promise at
> this season of the year, as old bulbs that have been buried
> in the ground all winter send up green shoots that burst into
> blossom, baby chicks hatch from chicken eggs, and bare trees
> send forth tiny green buds. To the small child, the basic atti-
> tude of joy and praise at Easter time is of prime importance.
> In later years, knowledge and belief can grow on this firm
> foundation, but the attitude of wonder and joy at Easter is
> what is most needed in the life of a small child.[8]

Using bright colors and dyeing Easter eggs are good ways to
emphasize new life to young children. Our parish always gives out
helium balloons to the children after the main Easter liturgy — a
great symbol of life and resurrection!

TRUST AND THE EXPERIENCE OF LOVE

Because trust, the feeling of security and safety, and the knowledge
that they are loved and cared for is so crucial for young children
in every aspect of their lives, it is also crucial for their relationship
with God. That trust can be nurtured by providing quiet time and
space (even if it's a very short time) where children can let their
hearts speak to God. Elise Boulding, a wonderful Quaker woman
and long-time peacemaker, puts it this way:

> The anchoring in the divine milieu that can take place in fam-
> ily settings depends on being able to conceive the home as a
> temple for listening, a place for individual solitude and group
> quiet. Since solitude and quiet are in general the last thing
> we look for at home, creative imagination has to be brought
> into play here. Designated quiet corners in the home, even
> when there is not enough space for a separate listening room;
> listening together in silence before meals, by candlelight for a

few minutes before bedtime, creates a kind of openness and attunement that is strangely akin to play, and yet delicately centered in a way that play is not. The openness is both horizontal and vertical — to God and to others. The family that sets a high value on "listening silence" helps put its members in touch with the inward teacher and nurturer of that spirit that takes away the occasion of war.[9]

Touching is extremely important in the building of trust — hugs, kisses, cuddles, sitting in someone's lap — all are concrete ways that children begin to understand the love of God. Since God is our loving Parent, children's experience of parental affection gives them a real taste of God's love.

Another important part of the trust foundation involves keeping our promises. If children know that we'll be where we say we'll be and that we'll do what we tell them we'll do, they have a glimpse of the faithfulness of God. How many times have we heard a child say, with utter disappointment, "But, you said...." Our fidelity, whether it is in reading a promised story or waiting on a street corner, is an anchor that they need emotionally and spiritually.

One last dimension of trust involves the child's name. "Yahweh called me from my mother's womb, Yahweh pronounced my name." How important to children are their names! How proud they are when they tell you their name and when they can write their name! Our respect for their name, never belittling it in any way and commenting at times on how much we like it, is crucial for children. We need to tell them for whom they were named; that is part of their own story. The story, however, does not always come out the way we intend. A story from our own family's history pointed that out to us.

It was our turn to host the home liturgy for our family support group. Since it was the first week of November, we chose as a theme "All Saints — Becoming Saints through Service." We had called the other three families and asked them to prepare their children to tell the stories of their own saints, or persons for whom they were named, during Mass. We also invited a friend from the Catholic Worker house to tell us about her work and how we might help.

At dinner the night before, we talked with our children about their patrons. With Mother Teresa about to receive the Nobel

Peace Prize, everyone was interested in Theresa's great namesake in India. David, too, had an interesting story to tell. He was named for David Darst, a relative and early Vietnam-war draft resister, one of the Catonsville Nine.

Tommy, however, was more of a challenge. He informed us right away that he did not want to tell the story of "that one Thomas — he was the only one, after Jesus rose from the dead, who didn't come to the meeting!" (Missing meetings is seen as a grave matter in our family.) So we told him about Thomas More. We could tell we had hit on the right Thomas — at least as far as curiosity was concerned. While David was preoccupied with what they did with Thomas More's head, Tommy focused on why he lost his head. The recorded reasons did not seem sufficient justification for sacrificing one's head; Tommy was clearly in less than total admiration of Thomas More's practical judgment.

The next evening at Mass, Tommy was the last of the children to tell their stories. After faithfully recalling the highlights of Thomas More's life and death, he concluded, "But I wouldn't have done it!" Then there was a lovely irony. At that point in the Mass we put on a record and listened meditatively (through the laughter) to the St. Louis Jesuits singing "Be Not Afraid."

Even though our attempts do not always bear the immediate fruits that we intend, the efforts are worth it in themselves. I find myself often thinking of the image from the prophet Isaiah, "If you do away with the yoke, the clenched fist, the wicked word, if you give your bread to the hungry, and relief to the oppressed, . . . Yahweh will always guide you, giving you relief in desert places. Yahweh will give strength to your bones and you shall be like a watered garden, like a spring of water whose waters never run dry" (Isaiah 58:9–11).

Notes

1. "Teaching Us the Source of Joy," an interview with Sofia Cavalletti, *Sojourners,* January 1987, p. 23.
2. Dolores Curran, "Rediscovering the Child Within," *St. Anthony Messenger,* May 1986, p. 29.
3. "Teaching Us the Source of Joy," p. 22.
4. "Letter of Chief Seattle," as quoted in James McGinnis, *Bread and Justice* (New York: Paulist Press, 1979), pp. 322–323.
5. In Dorothy Dixon, *The Formative Years* (West Mystic, Conn.: Twenty-Third Publications, 1977), p. 87.

6. Camy Condon and James McGinnis, *Puppets for Peace* (St. Louis, Mo. : Institute for Peace and Justice, 1984), p. 29.

7. *Parenting for Peace and Justice Newsletter,* no. 10, Winter 1983, p. 2.

8. Dixon, *Formative Years,* p. 43.

9. Kathleen and James McGinnis, *Parenting for Peace and Justice* (Maryknoll, N.Y. : Orbis Books, 1981), p. 116.

Resources

The resources recommended in these pages are divided into books to be read with children and books for adult background reading. They have been grouped according to chapters, although some of the books will be useful resources when dealing with the themes of several of the chapters.

Chapter 1: Foundation Blocks

Children's Reading

George Ancona. *I Feel*. New York: E. P. Dutton, 1977. A wide range of emotions are dealt with in this book. Children can talk about what they see in the pictures and how they feel about them.

Joy Wilt Berry. *Let's Talk about Fighting*. Chicago: Children's Press, 1984. Discusses how quarrels and fights develop and explores alternatives.

Nancy Gurney. *The King, the Mice and the Cheese*. New York: Beginners Books, 1965. A fine help for young children to begin to understand sharing.

Munro Leaf. *The Story of Ferdinand*. New York: Viking Press, 1936. A classic for young readers. Ferdinand is a bull who enjoys sitting under a tree and smelling flowers. He definitely does not like to fight.

Cornelia Lehn. Illustrated by Robert W. Regier. *The Sun and the Wind: An Aesop Fable Retold*. Newton, Kans.: Faith and Life Press, 1983. A beautifully illustrated fable. The sun proves to the wind that love is stronger than force.

Eda LeShan. Illustrated by Lisl Weil. *What Makes Me Feel This Way? Growing Up with Human Emotions*. New York: Collier Books, 1972. Provides help in recognizing emotions and identifying their causes and offers suggestions for managing our feelings.

Leo Lionni. *The Alphabet Tree.* New York: Pantheon, 1968. With the help of the word-bug, the letters of the alphabet deal with their fears of the wind and storms by grouping themselves into words for safety. The words are peace words.

Elberta H. Stone. Illustrated by Margery W. Brown. *I'm Glad I'm Me.* New York: G.P. Putnam's Sons, 1971. Intended to build self-concept. A young Black child speaks of the things "he'd like to be" (tree, bird, cloud, etc.) and ends by saying "I'm glad I'm me." Charcoal illustrations, rich in detail, add a sense of dignity to the story.

William Wondriska. *All the Animals Were Angry.* New York: Holt, Rinehart and Winston, 1970. A dove tells the quarreling animals that she loves them all.

Taro Yashima. *Crow Boy.* New York: Penguin Books, 1976. This sensitive story, which takes place in a Japanese setting, is about a universal experience of childhood, the struggle to gain acceptance. Includes some highlights of Japanese culture.

Charlotte Zolotow. *The Hating Book.* New York: Harper & Row, 1969. On friendship and talking through problems. A little girl discovers that she can communicate with someone she had "hated."

Adult Reading

Elizabeth Crary. *Kids Can Cooperate.* Seattle, Wash.: Parenting Press, 1983. Parents and teachers can benefit from the practical activities in this book, all focused on how to encourage children to cooperate.

Dolores Curran. *Stress and the Healthy Family.* Minneapolis: Winston Press, 1985. An important look at how healthy families learn to deal with conflicts and to cooperate.

Adele Faber and Elain Mazlish. *How to Talk So Kids Will Listen.* New York: Avon Publishing Company, 1980. Actual samples of family dialogue, warm and humorous.

Alvyn M. Freed. *Transactional Analysis for Tots.* Jalmar Press Inc. (45 Hitching Post Dr., Rolling Hills Estates, CA 90274), vol. 1, 1973; vol. 2, 1980. TA for Tots simplifies the basic ideas of Transactional Analysis and is geared to the pre-school level. The purpose is to assure children that they are OK, the first step in inoculating them against an environment that leads to destructive life patterns.

H. Stephen Glenn. *Strengthening the Family.* Bethesda, Md.: Potomac Press, 1981. This pamphlet contains practical ideas for helping children realize connections between chosen behavior and consequences.

Stephanie Judson. *A Manual on Nonviolence and Children.* Nonviolence and Children Program, Friends Peace Committee (1515 Cherry St.,

Philadelphia, PA 19102), 1977. A wealth of games, techniques, observations, and insights on developing nonviolence in children, especially pre-school and elementary school. Also available from New Society Publishers, 4722 Baltimore Ave., Philadelphia, PA 19142.

Eda LeShan. *When Your Child Drives You Crazy.* New York: St. Martin's Press, 1985. Warm anecdotes fill this book of practical advice on parenting from the "mother of parenting education."

Elizabeth Loescher. *How to Avoid World War III at Home.* Cornerstone (920 Emerson St., Denver, CO 80218), 1986. Concrete suggestions about how to handle conflict in the family.

Mark Ozer, M.D. *The Ozer Method.* New York: William Morrow Company, 1981. Represented a breakthrough in problem-solving ideas for parents and children.

Priscilla Prutzman et al. from the Children's Creative Response to Conflict Program. *The Friendly Classroom for a Small Planet.* Wayne, N.J.: Avery Publishing Company, 1978. This workbook for elementary teachers and parents contains affirmation exercises, practice activities for teaching creative problem solving, and conflict resolution ideas.

Sue Spayth Riley. *How to Generate Values in Young Children.* Washington, D.C.: National Association for the Education of Young Children, 1984. Examines the roots of value development, especially the values of integrity, honesty, individuality, self-confidence, and wisdom.

Charles Smith. *Promoting the Social Development of Young Children.* Palo Alto, Calif.: Mayfield Publishing Company, 1982. The development of personal and social skills, e.g., empathy, friendship, cooperation, conflict resolution, is detailed.

Chapter 2:
We're All Different! : Healthy Racial Attitudes

Children's Reading

(The numbers in parentheses at the end of the listings refer to the following four categories: (1) They present authentic information about elements of different cultures; (2) they directly counter racial stereotypes; (3) they depict children and/or adults of different racial/cultural groups in non-stereotypic ways in everyday situations and settings; (4) they offer positive role models of heroes from different racial/cultural groups. Some of the books include several of these elements, some only one.)

Annie and Julee. *Brown Spices ABC Book: A Great Coloring Book for Boys and Girls.* Brown Spices Publishing Co. (P.O. Box 29397, Washington, DC 20017-0397), 1984. An imaginative coloring book that celebrates the unity of Black families. (1, 2)

Mary Atkinson. *Maria Teresa.* Chapel Hill, N.C. : Lollipop Power, 1979. After a Spanish-speaking girl moves, it is difficult getting used to her new non-Hispanic environment. Her puppet sheep helps her make new friends. (3)

Charles Blood and Martin Link. *The Goat in the Rug.* New York: Parents Magazine Press, 1976. A delightful, fanciful tale told by a goat. An interesting way to explain the Navajo art of weaving to young children. (1)

Muriel Feelings. Illustrated by Tom Feelings. *Jambo Means Hello: Swahili Alphabet Book.* New York: Dial Press, 1974. An introduction to Swahili words. The illustrations are outstanding and evoke warmth and dignity. (1, 2)

Muriel Feelings. Illustrated by Tom Feelings. *Moja Means One: Swahili Counting Book.* New York: Dial Press, 1971. The reader is given an introduction to counting from one to ten in Swahili. The illustrations are exceptional. Both of the Feelings's books help to dispel any stereotypes children have about the fearsomeness of Africa and African people. (1, 2)

Eloise Greenfield. Illustrated by Moneta Barnett. *First Pink Light.* New York: Thomas Y. Crowell, 1976. Greenfield and Barnett team up to present a warm, enjoyable story of a small boy's desire to stay up until his daddy gets home. The reader can't help but be drawn into the love in the family. (2, 3)

Eloise Greenfield. Illustrated by Diane and Leo Dillon. *Honey, I Love and Other Love Poems.* New York: Thomas Y. Crowell, 1978. Beautiful illustrations, filled with sensitivity and pride, set off this collection. The poems cover a range of experiences, people, and emotions springing directly from a child's everyday life. Many of the themes would be understandable by pre-schoolers. (3)

Eloise Greenfield. *Rosa Parks.* New York: Thomas J. Crowell Company, 1973. This book sensitively depicts the indignities endured by Black people in our recent past and the quiet courage of Rosa Parks, "the Mother of the Civil Rights Movement," in bravely claiming her rights. (2, 4)

Juanita Havill. Illustrated by Anne Sibley O'Brien. *Jamaica's Find.* New York: Houghton Mifflin, 1986. This picture book deals with a common, everyday experience — deciding about returning something that has been found — in the context of a warm, loving Black family. (3)

Elizabeth S. Hill. *Evan's Corner.* New York: Holt, Rinehart and Winston, 1967. Evan's mother helps him establish a place of his own in their crowded apartment while also helping him to understand his little brother's need. (3)

Nigel Hunter. Illustrated by Richard Hook. *Martin Luther King, Jr.* New York: The Bookwright Press, 1986. Beautiful illustrations and photographs enliven this biography of King. (4)

Hattie Jones, ed. Illustrated by Robert Andrew Parker. *The Trees Stand Shining.* New York: Dial Press, 1971. A fine collection of Native American poetry for children. The selections are good for reading aloud. Beautiful watercolor illustrations. (1)

Robert Kraus. *The Rabbit Brothers.* New York: Anti-Defamation League of B'nai B'rith. This delightful book about two rabbits explains clearly the follies of prejudice. (2)

Leslie Jones Little and Eloise Greenfield. Illustrated by Carole Byard. *I Can Do It by Myself.* Scranton, Pa.: Thomas Y. Crowell, 1978. A warm story of a small boy's determination to get his mother's birthday present "by himself." (3)

Cruz Martel. *Yagua Days.* New York: Dial Press, 1976. A Puerto Rican boy living in the U.S. goes to visit his parents' hometown in Puerto Rico. Besides a simple description of "yagua days," the book deals with stereotyping of physical appearance. (1, 2)

Gerald McDermott. *Arrow to the Sun: A Pueblo Indian Myth.* New York: Viking, 1975. A folk tale strikingly illustrated in bold colors. (1)

Betty Miles. *Around and Around Love.* New York: Alfred A. Knopf, 1975. A wonderful book, with beautiful black and white photos. Shows love as valid in all ways, between all kinds of people. Good multicultural mix in the photos. (3)

Norma Simon. Illustrated by Dora Leder. *Why Am I Different?* Chicago: Albert Whitman & Co., 1976. Differences in physical make-up, personality, and culture are presented to give children an understanding of others. (2, 3)

Adult Reading

Council on Interracial Books for Children *Bulletin.* (1841 Broadway, New York, NY 10023). "Children, Race & Racism: How Race Awareness Develops," vol. 11, nos. 3–4 (1980). This special issue deals with ways to help children develop positive attitudes about themselves and others, how to help children deal with racist name-calling, and how race awareness develops. A thought-provoking resource for parents of all racial groups. A subscription to the *Bulletin* is $14/year for individuals and $20/year for institutions.

Council on Interracial Books for Children *Bulletin.* "Countering Bias in Early Childhood Education," vol. 14, nos. 7–8 (1983). This issue deals with racism, sexism, and handicapism as they relate to young children. An invaluable resource.

Mary Ellen Goodman. *Race Awareness in Young Children.* New York: Collier Books, 1964. A cultural anthropologist's study of how racial attitudes begin to form in four-year-olds. It still ranks as one of the most important research studies in the area and is excellent background reading for parents.

Dr. Phyllis Harrison-Ross and Barbara Wyden. *The Black Child.* New York: Berkley Publishing Corporation, 1973. An exceptionally enlightening parenting manual, valuable for Black parents and others as well.

Judy Katz. *White Awareness: Handbook for Anti-Racist Training.* University of Oklahoma Press, 1978. Contains useful activities for adult groups learning about racism.

Louis L. Knowles and Kenneth Prewitt, eds. *Institutional Racism in America.* Englewood Cliffs, N.J.: Prentice-Hall, 1969. This classic gives a basic explanation of the institutional dimension of racism.

Herbert Kohl. *Growing with Your Children.* Boston: Little, Brown and Company, 1978. A parenting book that deals well with the issue of white children and racism. Kohl's basic premise is that "children first learn racism consciously or unconsciously from their parents." Gives specific suggestions about how to create healthy racial attitudes.

James and Kathleen McGinnis, et al. *Educating for Peace and Justice.* St. Louis: Institute for Peace and Justice, 1985. See Volume I, units on Multicultural Education and Racism. This manual is oriented toward teachers but has many suggestions that are immediately adaptable to the home.

The Multicultural Project for Communication and Education (678 Massachusetts Ave., P.O. Box 125, Cambridge, MA 02139). *Caring for Children in a Social Context: Eliminating Racism, Sexism and Other Patterns of Discrimination,* 1981. This pamphlet is an invaluable resource for parents and child-care workers. Helps in the recognition of discrimination and provides practical suggestions for combatting it.

William Ryan. *Blaming the Victim.* New York: Vintage Books, 1976. Explains how society blames the victims of racism and poverty for their "problems," rather than blaming its own policies.

Lois Stalvey. *The Education of a Wasp.* New York: Bantam Books, 1971. A personal view of a white person coming to an understanding of the realities of racism.

Resources   119

Lois Mark Stalvey. *Getting Ready*. New York: Bantam Books, 1974. A penetrating look at racism in a big city school system and how a family deals with it.

Filmstrip:

"Childcare Shapes the Future: Anti-Racist Strategies," Council on Interracial Books for Children, 1841 Broadway, New York, NY 10023. This filmstrip/tape resource explains clearly how racism affects very young children and offers strategies for change.

Chapter 3:
Growing Up Equal: Sex-Role Stereotyping

Children's Reading

(The letters after the books refer to the following: (A) men and women, boys and girls shown in activities often considered "untypical" for their sex; (B) women shown as achievers and in positions of authority; (C) people shown actively working against sexism.)

Molly Bang. *Ten, Nine, Eight*. New York: Greenwillow, 1983. A warm, nurturing Black father helps his daughter fall asleep. (A)

Eloise Greenfield. Illustrated by Carole Byard. *Grandmama's Joy*. New York: Putnam, 1980. When Rhondy's grandmama is forced to move because she can no longer pay the rent, Rhondy assures her all will be well because she still has her "joy" — Rhondy. (B)

Dianne Homan. Illustrated by Mary Heine. *In Christina's Toolbox*. Charlotte: Lollipop Power, 1981. An excellent introduction to tools, how they are used, and how to care for them. The last illustration shows Christina putting her toolbox next to her mother's. (A)

Rachel Isadora. *Max*. New York: Macmillan, 1977. Max is enthusiastic about joining his younger sister's ballet class in order to warm up for baseball. (A)

Peggy Kahn. Illustrated by Enola Johnson. *The Handy Girls Can Fix It*. New York: Random House, 1984. This enjoyable tale shows the flexibility of sex roles. Four girls set up a fix-it shop, becoming the envy of two boys. (A)

Inez Maury. Illustrated by Sandy Speidel; translated by Anna Munoz. *My Mother and I Are Growing Strong! Mi mamá y yo nos hacemos fuertes*. Stamford, Conn.: New Seed Press, 1978. A creative story about a growing bond between mother and daughter and their continuing love for the father of the family, who is in prison. (A, C)

Inez Maury. Illustrated by Lady McGrady. *My Mother the Mail Carrier?*
Mi Mamá la Cartera? Old Westbury, N.Y.: The Feminist Press,
1976. A bilingual story of the relationship between a five-year-old
and her single mother. The mother and child truly rejoice in each
other. (A)

Susan Pearson. *Everybody Knows That!* New York: Dial, 1978. Contains
amusing responses to typical sex-role stereotypes. (A, C)

Letty Cottin Pogrebin, ed. *Stories for Free Children.* New York: McGraw
Hill, 1982. A collection of non-sexist, multicultural stories based on
a *Ms.* magazine feature. Contains some for very young children. (A,
B, C)

Marlo Thomas. *Free to Be, You and Me.* New York: McGraw Hill, 1974.
This compilation of stories, poetry, songs, dialogues, and essays is
a delightful but serious introduction to the ways sexism limits the
development of young men and women. It is especially valuable for
young children, but will be enjoyed by all ages. (A, C)

Vera B. Williams. *A Chair for My Mother.* New York: Greenwillow, 1982.
This picture book about a warm, loving extended working-class
family counteracts stereotypes. (A)

Vera B. Williams. *Something Special for Me.* New York: Greenwillow,
1983. Portrays a close, extended family whose small savings in a jar
will provide a birthday present for the little girl. Attempts to make
the reader sensitive to the struggles and decisions inherent in being
poor, while not romanticizing poverty. (A)

Adult Reading

Carrie Carmichael. *Non-Sexist Childraising.* Boston: Beacon Press, 1977.
Thought-provoking issues raised, from participatory childbirth to
sexism in schools.

Merle Froschl and Barbara Sprung, eds. *Beginning Equal: A Manual
About Nonsexist Childrearing for Infants and Toddlers.* New York:
Women's Action Alliance Inc. and the Pre-School Association, Inc.,
1983. Developed by Beginning Equal, the Project on Nonsexist
Childrearing for Infants and Toddlers. Combines theory with workshop materials, all geared toward awareness and action about sex-
role stereotyping in the earliest years.

Letty Cottin Pogrebin. *Growing Up Free: Raising Your Child in the '80s.*
New York: McGraw-Hill, 1980. Essential background reading for
teachers and parents, with a wealth of insights about how to deal
with sex-role stereotyping in everyday life.

June Shapiro, Sylvia Kramer, and Catherine Hunerberg. *Equal Their
Chances: Children's Activities for Non-Sexist Learning.* Englewood

Cliffs, N.J.: Prentice Hall, 1981. This book focuses on what educators and parents can do to make sex equity a part of school life.
Includes activities for all age levels.

Barbara Sprung, ed. *Perspectives on Non-Sexist Early Childhood Education.* New York: Teachers College Press, 1978. This book is a series
of readings that are valuable for people in early childhood education. Includes a list of resources.

Jessie Wenning and Sheli Wortis. *Made by Human Hands: A Curriculum
for Teaching Young Children About Work and Working People.* The
Multicultural Project for Communication and Education, Inc. (71
Cherry St., Cambridge, MA 02139), 1985. This booklet is full of
activity suggestions, as well as resources for making the world of
work more meaningful to very young children.

Filmstrip:

"Childcare Shapes the Future: Anti-Sexist Strategies." Council on Interracial Books for Children, 1841 Broadway, New York, NY 10023.
This filmstrip/tape set deals with sexism as it affects our treatment
of the very young, with specific strategies to overcome sexism.

Chapter 4: Respect for All:
Older People and People with Disabilities

Children's Reading

Lucille Clifton. Illustrated by Thomas DeGrazia. *My Friend Jacob.* New
York: Harper & Row, 1980. A wonderful story about a truly mutual
friendship between a young Black child and a white teen-ager who
is mentally retarded.

Helen Coutant. Illustrated by Bo-Dinh. *First Snow.* New York: Alfred
A. Knopf, 1974. This story of a small Vietnamese girl's relationship with her grandmother and the experience of her grandmother's
death is full of gentleness and warmth.

Eloise Greenfield. Illustrated by George Ford. *Darlene.* New York:
Methuen, 1980. A disabled girl enters into the fun while on a visit
to her uncle and cousin.

Lorraine Henriod. Illustrated by Christa Chevalier. *Grandma's Wheelchair.* Chicago: Albert Whitman, 1982. A delightful, fun-filled book
in which the active Grandma uses her wheelchair simply as an aid
for getting around.

Miska Miles. Illustrated by Peter Parnall. *Annie and the Old One.*
Boston: Little, Brown, 1971. Through her grandmother, a respected

Navajo elder, Annie learns a valuable lesson about growth, change, and death.

Philip Newth. *Roly Goes Exploring.* Philomil Books (200 Madison Ave., New York, NY 10016), 1981. An ingenious book, done both in braille and in large print, good for developing an understanding of shapes.

Jeanne Whitehouse Peterson. Illustrated by Deborah Ray. *I Have a Sister: My Sister Is Deaf.* New York: Harper & Row, 1977. Even though done from a hearing person's perspective, this book is more accurate than most.

Berenice Rabe. Illustrated by Lillian Hoban. *The Balancing Girl.* New York: Dutton, 1981. Presents a child in a wheelchair as a capable person.

Margaret Reuter. Photos by Philip Lanier. *My Mother Is Blind.* Chicago: Childrens Press, 1979. After his mother loses her vision, a young child describes her rehabilitation process in a way that could stimulate good discussion.

Jane Resh Thomas. Illustrated by Emily Arnold McCully. *Wheels.* New York: Clarion Books, 1986. Five-year-old Elliot learns something about competition with the help of his grandfather.

Betty Ren Wright. Illustrated by Helen Cogancherry. *My Sister Is Different.* Raintree (205 Highland Ave., Milwaukee, WI 53203), 1981. Can help to generate understanding and respect for people with developmental disabilities.

Charlotte Zolotow. Illustrated by William Pene Du Bois. *My Grandson Lew.* New York: Harper & Row, 1974. Lewis shares his happy memories of his grandfather with his mother — "He gave me eye-hugs. . . . "

Adult Reading

Ellen Barnes, Carol Berrigan, and Douglas Biklen. *What's the Difference? Teaching Positive Attitudes Toward People with Disabilities.* Human Policy Press (P.O. Box 127, University Station, Syracuse, NY 13210), 1978. This book of classroom activities suggests over ninety ways for teachers to help students develop greater familiarity with and understanding of their disabled peers.

Dr. Robert N. Butler. *Why Survive? Being Old in America.* New York: Harper & Row, 1975. In this angry and thoroughly documented book, a noted gerontologist and psychiatrist balances the grim reality of what it is like to be old in the U.S. against the pieties that deny that reality.

Council on Interracial Books for Children *Bulletin* (1841 Broadway, New York, NY 10023). "Handicapism in Children's Books," vol. 8, nos.

6–7 (1977). A special issue on handicapism that is filled with data, teaching suggestions, and helpful resources.

Council on Interracial Books for Children *Bulletin* (1841 Broadway, New York, NY 10023). "Ageism in Children's Books," vol. 8, nos. 6–7 (1976). A special issue on Ageism. This volume and the previous listing are still essential reading.

Bernard Ikeler. *Parenting Your Disabled Child.* Philadelphia: Westminster Press, 1986. The author shares personal concrete insights, meaningful both to parents of disabled children and to others.

Richard O. Ulin. *Teaching and Learning About Aging.* Washington, D.C.: NEA Publications, 1982. Information on various aspects of the aging process and recent developments in curricula that deal with aging.

Chapter 5:
Violence and Peace: Here and Around the World

Children's Reading

Tomie de Paola. *The Hunter and the Animals.* Northville, Mich.: Holiday House, 1981. A wordless story in stylized detail of a forest of peaceful animals who help their enemy, the hunter. He then breaks his gun to show that he will no longer try to kill them.

Eloise Greenfield. Illustrated by Carole Byard. *African Dream.* Scranton, Pa.: John Day Co., 1977. The soft, flowing illustrations in this book are very fitting for a story about a Black child's dream trip to "Africa of long ago." Good linkage between Black Americans and their African roots.

Jan Hogan. Illustrated by Jeanine Wine. *Gladdys Makes Peace.* Elgin, Ill.: Brethren Press, 1985. This simply written biography of a peace educator, Gladdys Muir, emphasizes personal responsibility in peacemaking.

Margo Humphrey. *The River That Gave Gifts.* San Francisco: Children's Book Press, 1978. In this Afro-American story, four children in an African village make special gifts for an elder who is going blind.

Jeanne M. Lee. *Toad Is the Uncle of Heaven.* New York: Holt, Rinehart, & Winston, 1985. An amusing Vietnamese folktale about how the ugly toad cooperated with other animals to save the earth.

Cornelia Lehn. *Peace Be with You.* Newton, Kans.: Faith and Life Press, 1980. In these fifty-nine stories of peace heroes, there is humor and sadness, global sensitivity and next-door-neighbor vignettes, the young and the elderly, happy endings and sad. Each story is short enough to capture the attention of a young child but written maturely enough for an older person to appreciate.

Seymour Leichman. *The Boy Who Could Sing Pictures*. New York: Doubleday, 1968. The king is at war and doesn't realize the damage it is doing until the boy sings to him about the sadness he sees.

Anita Lobel. *Potatoes, Potatoes*. New York: Harper & Row, 1967. The story of a woman who refuses to take part in war. Her two sons join opposite armies and come home with their hungry armies to eat potatoes. This book clearly points out the futility of war and the hardships it creates.

Dorothy Morrison, Roma Dehi, Ronald M. Bazar. Illustrated by Nola Johnston. *We Can Do It*. Namchi United Enterprises (P.O. Box 33852, Station D, Vancouver, B.C., Canada V6J 4L6), 1985. This upbeat alphabet book describes all kinds of concrete actions people can take to work for world peace.

Hiawyn Oram. Illustrated by Satoshi Kitamina. *In the Attic*. New York: Holt, Rinehart and Winston, 1984. A wonderfully illustrated book that challenges children to look to their own creative powers for their sources of adventure.

Min Peak. *Aekyung's Dream*. San Francisco: Children's Book Press, 1978. A beautifully illustrated bilingual book tells the story of a young Korean girl, newly arrived in the United States, who finds strength in a dream about Korean history.

Kjell Ringi. *The Stranger*. New York: Random House, 1968. The reaction of a village to a stranger who is so tall his face can't be seen, but who becomes a friend to the villagers. Useful for discussing differences between people, enemies, stereotypes, aggression, war, peace, and communication.

Dr. Seuss. *The Butter Battle Book*. New York: Random House, 1984. A powerful statement about the military mentality, exposing the foolishness of the arms race.

Stanford Summers. *Wacky and His Fuddlejig*. Fiddlejig (Box 837, Times Square Station, New York, NY 10036), 1968, revised in 1980. The story concerns one of Santa's helpers who finds himself out of step with his co-workers in the military toy department. Finally he decides to quit, preferring to spend his time creating a toy that will appeal to a child's imagination.

Efua Sutherland. Photographs by Willis E. Bell. *Playtime in Africa*. New York: Atheneum, 1962. A prominent Ghanaian author invites the reader through both text and photography to join happy, bubbly children at play in a variety of settings and activities.

William Wondriska. *John, John Twilliger*. New York: Holt, Rinehart and Winston, 1966. The message is that dictators are human and reachable, as JJ makes friends with the dictatorial mayor and the town changes drastically.

Sofia Zaramboulke. *Irene.* Washington, D.C.! Tee Loftin Publishers, 1979. From Educators for Social Responsibility. A beautifully illustrated fable about peace. The book also includes a play for young children.

Claudia Zaslavsky. Illustrated by Jerry Pinkney. *Count on Your Fingers African Style.* New York: Thomas Y. Crowell, 1980. Simple text and engaging illustrations teach numbers and counting and also give a glimpse of several African peoples.

Jacob Zim. *My Shalom, My Peace.* St. Louis: McGraw-Hill, Sabra Books, 1975. A moving collection of paintings and poems on the theme of peace by Arab and Jewish children.

Adult Reading

William Nancy Carlsson-Paige and Diane E. Levin. *Helping Young Children Understand Peace, War, and the Nuclear Threat.* Washington, D.C.: National Association for the Education of Young Children, 1985. This booklet combines theory and practical suggestions. Helpful for teachers and parents.

Kate Cloud, Ellie Deegan, Adia Evans, Hayat Iman, and Barbara Signer. *Watermelons Not War! A Support Book for Parenting in the Nuclear Age.* Philadelphia: New Society, 1984. An attractive book that offers data on nuclear realities as well as common-sense advice for parents on how to instill hope in children and in themselves.

Camy Condon. *Puppets for Peace* and *Global Family Puppets.* St. Louis: Institute for Peace and Justice, 1984. These two program guides contain scripts and activities. The first deals with resolving conflict nonviolently and how children can work for world peace. The second helps children understand and challenge world hunger and live as members of a global family.

Susan Goldberg. *Facing the Nuclear Age: Parents and Children Together.* Toronto: Annick Press Ltd., 1985. An exceptionally useful resource answering the question "What Can We Do?"

Gerry and Pat Mische. *Toward a Human World Order.* New York: Paulist Press, 1977. A clear analysis of present global realities and suggestions for citizen participation. An essential overview.

Terry Orlick. *The Cooperative Sports and Games Book: Challenge Without Competition.* New York: Pantheon Books, 1978. A wonderful resource of cooperative games, with one chapter devoted specifically to games for pre-schoolers.

Terry Orlick. *The Second Cooperative Sports and Games Book.* New York: Pantheon Books, 1982. This sequel to Orlick's first book contains more games plus co-operative games from a variety of cultures.

William and Mary Wicker Van Ornum. *Talking to Children About Nuclear War*. New York: Continuum, 1984. Practical advice about a tough issue, including specific suggestions for very young children.

Video:

Buster and Me, "Getting Active." Produced by Christina Metcalf for KRON-TV, 1983. Distributed by Educational Film and Video Project, 1529 Josephine St., Berkeley, CA 94703. An audio-visual resource dealing with children's nuclear fears and possibilities for hope. Uses puppets in a charming way. Available in 3/4 inch, VHS, and BETA formats.

Chapter 6: Rooted in Faith

Children's Reading

Neal Boehlke. Illustrated by Susan Morries. *Zacchaeus Meets the Savior*. St. Louis: Arch Books, Concordia Publishing House, 1980. The well-known story of the complete change in the life of the publican Zacchaeus because of his encounter with Christ.

Carol Greene. Illustrated by Betty Wind. *The Easter Women*. St. Louis: Arch Books, Concordia Publishing House, 1987. The "Easter Women's" story is told in a simple and charming way, especially the story of Mary Magdalen.

Carol Greene. Illustrated by Betty Wind. *The Innkeeper's Daughter*. St. Louis: Arch Books, Concordia Publishing House, 1973. Little Abigail is transformed by the birth of Christ at her family's inn.

Carol Greene. Illustrated by Alice Hausner. *Kiri and the First Easter*. St. Louis: Arch Books, Concordia, 1972. A delightful story about a young boy who witnessed the death and resurrection of Christ.

Jan Johnson. Illustrated by Kathryn E. Shoemaker. *Brother Francis*. Minneapolis: Winston Press, Inc., 1977. An appealing biography of one of the great peace heroes, Francis of Assisi.

Mervin Marquardt. Illustrated by Obata Designs, Alice Hausner. *The Prisoner Who Freed Others*. St. Louis: Arch Books, Concordia Publishing House, 1974. Julie is a fictional character who meets the Apostle Paul and learns how much people need other people and how much they need God.

Dolores Ready. Illustrated by Rich Cooley. *The Boy Who Made His Pennies Go a Long Way*. Minneapolis: Winston Press, 1977. Compassion and a deep sense of caring for the poor come through strongly in this biography of Martin de Porres.

Mary Warren. Illustrated by Jim Roberts. *The Great Escape*. St. Louis:
Arch Books, Concordia Publishing House, 1973. A child's version
of the exodus from Egypt.
E. Elaine Watson. Illustrated by Barbara J. Pride. *My Feet Are for
Walking*. Cincinnati: The Standard Publishing Company, 1986. This
bright, cheery book builds a sense of gratitude for all that we have —
feet, hands, eyes, ears, etc.

Adult Reading

Ronice E. Branding. *Peacemaking: The Journey from Fear to Love*. St.
Louis: Christian Board of Publication, 1987. The spirituality of
peacemaking in our own lives, as well as the lives of our congre-
gations, is explored. Filled with practical suggestions.
Carol Dittbeiner. "The Pure Wonder of Young Lives." *Sojourners*, January 1987, pp. 21–25. Practical points about understanding and
enhancing the natural spirituality of young children.
Dorothy A. Dixon. *The Formative Years*. West Mystic, Conn.: Twenty-
Third Publications, 1977. The author's years of experience with
pre-schoolers are evident in this highly readable book. The chapter
on "Nurturing Spiritual Growth" is especially helpful.
Matthew Fox. *Original Blessing*. Santa Fe, N.M.: Bear & Company, 1983.
Called a "primer in creation spirituality," this book gives theory
and examples to explain a creation-centered spirituality, including
its social dimensions.
Kathleen and James McGinnis. *Parenting for Peace and Justice*. Maryknoll N.Y.: Orbis Books, 1981. Deals with the issues with a strong
faith emphasis.

Video:

Building Shalom Families. St. Louis: Institute for Peace and Justice,
1986. A comprehensive video program to assist families in dealing
with peace and justice issues. Designed within a Christian context.